Fairy Bridemother's

Wedding Handbook

How to Plan Your Dream Wedding
without Busting Your Budget or
Alienating Friends & Family

MELINDA MORGAN

ACKNOWLEDGEMENTS

Many thanks to,
Caroline, Dawn, Lora and Alex
who have given me so much emotional
and creative support

to the Turners
for providing me solace and shelter
without even understanding why

and to my amazing parents
who have eternally modeled what to do
and what not do to in every couple situation

Without any of these mentioned, I would not have had
the confidence, finances, or solitude desperately needed
to produce this work that represents my passion

A special shout out to Dawn for editing this book, and to
Alex for being the driving force of the valuable videos
you will experience within the content.

**PLEASE VIEW THE
VIDEOS THAT ACCOMPANY
EACH CHAPTER**

**PLEASE
DOWNLOAD A QR/BARCODE
SCANNER TO VIEW THE VIDEOS ON
YOUR SMARTPHONE**

**LOOK FOR QR SYMBOL
THROUGHOUT THE BOOK
AND CLICK FOR
EDUCATIONAL ENTERTAINMENT**

For future education and entertainment,
please subscribe to the YouTube
channel.

BUT FIRST.....
A FEW DISCLAIMERS

Fairy Bridemother is a purely fictitious character developed from the mind of an actual seasoned wedding designer and planner whose experience spans three decades.

Fairy Bridemother is an amazingly flamboyant and over-exaggerated entertainer.

The content of this book cannot leap off the page and magically create a successful wedding *for* you.

However, if you apply all of the advice and allow your imagination to guide you, it could be as if you waved your own magic wand and made it magically happen.

WHY THIS BOOK WAS WRITTEN:

○ There is just too much chaos surrounding the typical wedding today
○ I've witnessed Brides who could not decide on a gown until everything else was done and then felt cornered by their other choices
○ I've watched brides suffer who have no vision, no voice, and get bullied into choices they never wanted
○ Brides need to know *how* to make everything look as great as possible on any budget
○ The zillas who feel they have to get all nasty to get what they want better communication
○ Brides who don't understand all the things that have to be in done – and in what order – to bring a successful event to life
○ Because I have simply endured too many cheesy check-list weddings

Be Assertive!   Be Proactive!

Most of these problems can be resolved by bolstering your communication skills and helping you have a clear vision of what you would like for your big day!

If you are happy with all of your decisions, everybody else is going to be happy all around you as well. So just relax and celebrate the love that you share with this amazing person to whom you are now engaged. Let your planning be an extension of that love and all the wonderful things that made it happen in the first place.

Now, I must confess that do I love all the new technologies, gadgetries, and gizmos for the more modern weddings and all the elements that make up the traditional wedding as well, however, don't think that just because you sign up for all sorts of expensive little gadgets that your wedding will be fabulous. Remember, YOU are what make your wedding fabulous. Well, you and that wonderful soon-to-be spouse of yours that is.

It sometimes troubles me when I hear, "I want as traditional a wedding as possible" but what does that really mean? That you want to go down some checklist of a lot of long-standing "traditions" derived from decades, centuries (or longer) of superstitions that have metamorphosized into more palatable activities for today's society. You see, I know where these "traditions" come from and although *I* don't particularly care for some of their origins, (if you want to know the history, check out the bonus section of this book) however some of the changes to these "traditions" have become more fun.

That said, I believe that everyone has the right to choose whatever they want for their big day – as long as they don't completely make everyone around them miserable.....

I believe:

- ♥ An educated bride is a happier bride.
- ♥ Every bride deserves to look and feel like a million dollars on her big day.

♥ The wedding day should represent the bride, her groom, and their values as a couple.

♥ AND, most of all, I believe in YOU. I believe that *every* bride can have their own little bridal utopia simply by implementing all the things you will learn in this book.

Happy planning – and execution – dear bride! (remember to make sure **_you_** are not the person people want to execute by your wedding day…)

Fairy Bridemother

Table of Contents

BONUS!

Go to www.Fairy-Bridemother.com/bonus to download
or scan this

15 Wedding Myths,
Superstitions & Traditions

YOUR STYLE

So, this is where we start! Ready?! Well, ready or not, here we go…..

You are you, and there is no other like you. There are no two people alike and there are no two weddings alike – or at least there shouldn't be two weddings alike… Your wedding should be a reflection of you, your personality, style, and taste. Just remember, as you start your journey, all of these things could potentially change somewhat. You want to make sure that you don't get all married to any one specific element for your big day (except your man that is) or you will miss all the fun the metamorphosis the process of planning your wedding brings to your life.

As with any major, crazy, massive, life-altering event, on the other side you will be a different you. Make sure this process is improving your outlook, skills, and talents and not causing your beautiful light to deteriorate or turn you will into a monster – that is where those not-so-mythological zillas come from.

Your wonderful man asked *you* to marry him for a reason – a big one – you are you. Stay the *"you"* he fell for. Only allow growth – of your soul, not your hips.

1

Just allow this process to continue to grow your communication skills through this somewhat traumatic thing we call wedding planning, and he will love you all the more as you mature into an amazing life partner and wife. Now don't get all bra-burning on me when I say that word. Remember, you said "yes" to be someone's wife. I'm just helping you get to the altar in style!

Now, as we begin, I want you to take a moment and consider some things. Write down ideas about celebrating your union.

Begin forming your style or overall vision for your wedding with just a few words that describe the two of you as a couple as well as for each of you as individuals.

Below, we will go through finding the best way to bring these words to life so you can have an event to remember for the rest of your lives.

But first, here are some reasons "why" you are about to do this deep dive into your psyche and step out of your comfort zone.

Benefits:

When you create a clear vision for your wedding, your party and parents have the opportunity to "buy in" to that vision and help you bring it into reality

You have the perfect – non-confrontational – argument for why you do or don't want certain things for your day, gown, colors, bridesmaids, or groomsmen

You get to avoid a bunch of drama!

Drama is what derails most brides from their intended destination. A couple with a lack of clear vision or proper communication can be tossed about in the sea of what the parents or friends want without a life raft – which can leave hard feelings between the couple or in-laws and not a great way to start your union.

Every decision needs to flow out from the vision you create. Now this does not mean "don't be flexible."

This vision allows you to weave the suggestions from others that you *like* into the day you are creating with your "team." Yes, I said TEAM! It takes more than one person to pull off any major event – so start thinking in that direction right now!

Resist the temptation to respond immediately as to whether you like or do not like an idea.

Allow your loved one to use all their words on the subject, tell them when they are finished that you appreciate them sharing this idea with you, and you'll think about their suggestion or advice or discuss that idea with your fiancé.

Why? you ask? Because we want the people closest to us to feel validated – whether you use their idea or not.

Remember, your parents or surrogate parents, future in-laws, bridesmaids, groomsmen, other friends and family are your "TEAM". Mostly, people just want to help or be a significant part of your love/relationship/big day in some way.

Ok, others want to hijack your day for their own ideas and live out their own fantasies vicariously through you. But, you will figure out who-is-who in the process. Just ride the wave and allow the good little helper fairies to help. Just smile and nod graciously at the ones who seem to want to take over – and move on.

I digress – getting back on track. But most people are going to support you in your vision if you make your vision clear to yourself as well as communicate it to others.

I don't care if you have been fantasizing about your wedding since you were five or pinned a million pictures of what you think you want on your favorite virtual pinboard, you need a clear, communicate-able vision which will visibly define your style to others **and keep you grounded**.

Working to create this vision will provide the proper boundaries you can use to deflate any arguments before they can even begin!!!

This segment will take you a little while to complete, but please take the time to do this part prior to moving along to other topics. It will greatly benefit you. So, here come the questions...

Disclaimer:

Obviously, if you are just getting to read this after you

have already purchased items for your big day, still take the time to do this segment and include a picture of the items you have already purchased with a newly created statement for that item under the appropriate descriptive word.

You may need to return a few items if they don't exactly line up with your overall vision. If you cannot return the items, at least clearly communicate to your helpers "how" you could still use the items you already have to "make" them work.

It is clearly beneficial to stop at this point and assess everything now before making more purchases.

Create your Vision

FIRST! Find out if your groom wants to be involved on any level in creating this vision WITH you. WITH is the operative word here.

If you are doing this TOGETHER, make sure that you discuss **all** the main parts – color scheme, theme, location, food, dancing, and music. You can still allow his input largely into this big event and work in everything else you want. Men usually don't want to get very involved in the minutia of the event.

BUT, many **do** want to feel as though they have a say in what happens without actually having to do any of the details themselves.

There is later on how to ask specific questions to know if

he really wants involvement and on what level. If not, it is all up to you. Now don't be frightened little bride. That's a good thing. That means this wonderful whirlwind is *all yours*!

Think of it......This is *probably* the last day of your life that you get to decide absolutely **everything** – so take full advantage of it.

Now, let's begin to pick your brain!

Write down your answers to the following questions under the words you wrote down to describe each of you and you as a couple (oh did you miss that part? – we are looking for the 2-5 words that best describe you as a couple and individuals):

How do you want your wedding to feel?

What is the overall essence, look, smell, feel of your day?

Is it vintage, rustic, modern, classic and traditional, edgy and non-traditional?

Do you want massive amounts or flowers or tons of candlelight?

Do you want a super-romantic feel, something casual and laidback, or over-the-top black tie?

DO NOT FEEL LIMITED BY THE ABOVE QUESTIONS: THESE ARE JUST TO GET YOUR BRAIN GOING. KEEP WRITING DOWN DESCRIPTIONS

OF YOUR THOUGHTS AND IMAGINATION

Now, identify **at least** five words that describe the day you envision and this will be the foundation of what your day will be built creating your event style.

Now, think for a moment about the words you have just written down. Under each word, write down at least two (but try for three) statements that paint a picture of what achieving that word looks like.

Example: You said "rustic". Describe what "rustic" means to you in visual terms. The ceremony would be in a field with lots of trees and the reception would be in a rustic barn. There would be lots of burlap, hay, and lace. The girls would carry daisies in their bouquets and wear flowers in their hair. I want to wear boots... I want <u>everyone</u> to wear boots. Etc......

Now, paste one or two pictures that reveal what you would like to achieve (at least to some level) under each of those statements. Now, this is going to be an *on-going* process until things are actually purchased and contracts are signed on venues.

IMPORTANT!!!!
DO NOT GO ANY FURTHER UNTIL YOU HAVE
COMPLETED THE ABOVE EXERCISES.
(with or without your man)
OTHERWISE, YOU WILL WASTE MONEY, TIME,
AND POSSIBLY SOME OF YOURSELF!

Also, re-address the above exercise of collecting visual

aids throughout this planning process – especially after you have nailed down your dress and your venue. You may need to adjust or throw your initial plan out the window and have to start over if the dress you fall madly in love with doesn't suit your overall plan.

That is why you choose your dress and venue prior to making any other solid financial choic-es.

Make certain that you find ways to make all the differing elements you would like to have for your special day flow together. If one doesn't fit and it is going to stick out like a sore thumb, you may need to toss it out and find another event to achieve that fun idea or theme – like a shower or bridesmaid luncheon.

Once you purchase items and have the venues (but re-member, we haven't gotten there just yet) put pictures of what you actually have purchased right next to the ideas of the vision you would like to achieve.

Ask yourself if these items will really help you achieve your goal.

If not, return them.

If so, keep the picture of them next to the inspiration photo you are trying to achieve.

Your items do not have to match any inspiration items exactly – especially if you are on a strict budget.

This is not about comparing yourself, talents, or items to a photo-shopped massively-expensive vision.

This exercise is only about keeping yourself grounded in your choices, to create the wedding of your dreams that reflect your personal uniqueness and desires – and keep everything within your budget.

Be bold and be decisive about your final decisions – and then be happy. Use everything you purchase as building blocks toward your final vision and do away with ALL other options that do not flow with your outlined vision!

ANNOUNCING

So far, only you and your new fiancé know you're getting hitched (unless he had helpers)! So, this is really the only place this book will be touching the word "etiquette."

With our new technology, however, things can get a bit sticky for you if you post your exciting news on your *social network of choice* prior to notifying close friends and family members in person or at least with a phone call. The stickiness snowballs if you have not already introduced your soon-to-be spouse to these important people prior to such a monumental decision to unite.

Do NOT post a picture of your hand wearing your new sparkly ring on Facebook or change your status *until* you have told the important and proper people first.

This step or mis-step alone can make the people in your world feel very special or **very** devalued. It **is** still possible these days to contain the big news before it leaks out through social media.

Be aware of whom you need to tell first before any sort of social or formal announcement is made.

Usually if something gets out prematurely it is because You Leak It!

Now, unfortunately (I say that with a heavy sigh), en-gagement parties, or at least surprise announcements, have gone by the wayside in most of our modern unions, but I just love the idea of a good engagement party.

If you can keep a lid on the news, there is nothing quite like bringing together two families and intimate friends under one roof to announce the exciting news! Even if you have to tell them to get them there, tell them to keep it to themselves because it is a surprise. A big an-nouncement like this can just be fun-filled magic!

Caveat: if some of your most-significant people live out of town, make the call together to tell them the news and then if there are local people, then have the party. You can even include your out-of-town people in the party on some of that great new technology.

This is also a good way to spread some good cheer in case any damage has already been done. Make sure to invite parents, siblings, and include people that you would like considered for attendants at your wedding that your betrothed or family may not already know.

Have a small cocktail party at your home with a request to dress up for the special occasion. And turn this into an opportunity to thank your families and friends in ad-vance for their support and love. Take time to introduce everyone to everyone and see how people are going to get along at their first meeting. This will help to prepare yourself if you need to keep two valuable assets separated for the duration of the planning...

Even if all you can afford is cheez-whiz on crackers, this is a great way to get the news to the right people all at once or mend fences without feelings getting damaged further in the process.

Outside of making the big announcement, this is a great time to make small talk about potential plans, dates, and keep conversation light and moving. This is a very easy way to find out if either of your parents are already planning to make hefty contributions to the cause or if they are flat broke. In this day and age, never *expect* your parents to pay. Just be grateful if they do.

Take this time to formulate your teams for gown shopping, décor creators, vendor coordinators, and who knows whom so that you might get the best possible quality or deals and stretch your budget. In these thoughts, ask yourself who is the most supportive, who is trying to run the show, who really loves the ideas I'm throwing out in conversation, who is trying to just get their own way and live vicariously through my wedding? Be smart about who you let on what team – avoid drama magnets and drama makers.

Ask people, "Would you email that suggestion or information to me so I can look it over after the party?" This is a great way to keep things moving and not get bogged down into details. It keeps you from having to make notes, commit to anything prematurely, and you'll also find out who is going to be the most helpful or what things are important to each person. Let people help – if you feel their intentions are good.

If you print out these emails and put them in a categorized binder, you'll be prepared and not completely overwhelmed with the amount of information that could flow your way. This can be combined with your own research on vendors and the categorization will help you decide who to check out by phone and with whom to have face-to-face meetings to discuss potential contracts.

P.S. – put a big paper calendar out on a table or in the kitchen. Ask the people at the party to block out any time they have already planned to be out of town and place their name on that time block. This will help you plan special events and a wedding date a little easier.

Dream Team

Now, it is time to create your dream team. Show off your ring, change your status on your favorite social networks, etc. Talk to your friends, soon-to-be in-laws, family, potential wedding party, that person that just offered to help you out of the blue, etc.

Only talk in broad, non-descript or vague terms about what you'd like to accomplish based off the vision you have begun to create. See who buys into the excitement and recruit them as an ally.

Keep a list of people's names, email, and phone numbers that have offered to help in some way. There may come a time when you need something minor (or major) done just prior to or during the wedding day and you find yourself short-staffed.

These people are invaluable because they could help you address invitations, put favors together, hand out programs at the ceremony, etc. And if you have an extremely small budget they could help cut and serve cake, put out place cards, or help with day-of coordination.

Remember, you are running a volunteer organization during this process – Be nice to people! Be grateful they want to help you!

Be the Bride!

Have specific duties written out that are modified over the course of planning for your bridesmaids. If you keep everything realistic and well-defined, there are fewer hurt feelings, overworked individuals, and fewer arguments.

Have regular conversations with your bridesmaids *(we are getting to them)* about how things are coming. Make sure to be kind and patient, but constantly in communication so you can maintain your checklists as you formulate them.

It is nice to get all your bridesmaids together monthly, but if that's not feasible, don't stress if someone cannot make it. You cannot expect everyone else's lives to suddenly stop and only revolve around you.

You may be the bride that gets overwhelmed at too many lines on your checklist and need to categorize everything, or you may be the bride that doesn't feel like you have accomplished anything unless you see lots of items checked off.

Either way, just start writing out what you need to do or buy, get it done, and check it off. Just allow yourself enough time to accomplish the vision you have.

Then set the date!

You either need time to diy or lots money to pull off an elaborate wedding.

MANAGING REQUESTS AND DEMANDS

the groom, the parents, the siblings,
and the in-laws and the out-laws

This is a VERY important section.

Remember that most people don't know a lot about weddings until they get in the middle of them.

Parents and your groom will most likely want to guide you away from or towards certain things for their own reasons. It is best to listen with a concerned ear at their "in-general" and specific requests. Make little notes about them. This does not mean, however, that every single request has to be answered. It *does* mean you should at least listen.

Your wedding is what sets the stage for your new life together – not only with your groom, but with your new set of parents.

Understandably, they may be crazy. They may ask for you to allow more involvement than you would like. They may even ask for you to carry on certain traditions from their families that may seem foreign to you. Just listen to their requests. Discuss it with your groom and

17

decide later if you can meet these requests without sacrificing your personal taste, style, beliefs, or traditions.

Weddings don't really change. There has always been a couple either wanting to publicly show their love and affection for each other, or two families coming together for the sake of money or power. There aren't too many arranged marriages any more, but it still happens.

Many of the traditions that you thought you had to adhere to from yesteryear are over. The meanings have been muddled and replaced throughout the decades and when introduced today, some can feel cliché.

Does that mean you shouldn't do them, heavens no! It just means try not to feel like you *have to* do them in order to have a proper or even traditional wedding.

There is even a bonus section at the end of this book for the stories behind many traditions. You can decide if you want these things implemented in your day. And if you don't and come upon a critic, you can throw some history lesson at them to justify your choice (if you think they deserve a response to their un-asked-for critique in the first place).

So, on to the fun stuff!

Before reacting to anyone's requests or demands, just make notes. Seek to understand why they feel it is important to them, or even **if** it is important or was just a suggestion in passing with no real personal, familial or emotional bearing.

If a request or tradition has family history or emotional bearing, at least write it down and relay that you will put some thought into the request.

If you will write things down as you are having the conversation, you will find they will feel more validated and like you care.

If you find you can weave even one or a few things into your big celebration, you will have some life-long allies. There is a lot to be said for getting on the in-laws' good side if you aren't already there.

Make sure that if you decide to use someone's request or idea to write them a special note thanking them for their input and that you really appreciate them. You will have an ally for life – or at least for the duration of your planning.

Including Your Groom

Some grooms really want to avoid every possible involvement in planning "your" wedding, and then many want to be included in every decision because this big day is supposed to be a reflection of both of you as a couple.

Here are some questions to ask to see what level of involvement he would like to have as well as gauging his value of importance in certain areas.

Would you like to help me select a DJ for the reception or musicians for the ceremony?

Are there any specific songs that you would like played or banned from our big day?

How important to you is where we get married or have the reception? *If this is something he shows interest, put him in charge of scouting your dream wedding venue. And you can make some site visits together.*

Would you like for me to choose what you and your groomsmen are wearing or would you like to work together to select the ideal wedding outfits? *Maybe suggest a joint trip to the tux shop or discuss vintage alternatives.*

Are there any of your favorite drinks and food that you would like to be considered to be served for one of our events? *This could be at the rehearsal dinner, suggestions to the best man for the bachelor party, or even the reception. Find a place to make a few things fit. But make sure these things are important to him prior to making a lot of needless effort.*

Would you like to have a creative groom's cake that reflects *his interest*?

NEXT?

THE DRESS

Warning: Be careful who you take gown shopping. **Do not** take your whole family and all your bridesmaids! Do not take anyone who will bully you! Make sure only the people that will support your vision and sense of style are invited! And do not set back-to-back appointments to select dresses with your bridesmaid the same day as your gown unless your wedding is in the next three months (then only invite them to the bridesmaids' appointment)!

The Dress The Dress *The Dress*

I am certain you have heard the phrase *it's all about the dress*. Well, that is very true and very *not* true. Here is what I mean.

Call your local bridal stores and find out the price range of their gowns. If they are out of your budget, don't even make an appointment or reassess your budget before going.

Your dress shouldn't devour the entire budget for your wedding; however, your dress **is** the focal point for everything *in* your entire wedding, so DON'T SKIMP either!

This will be the most photographed garment you've ever worn – ever!

And, you are the one that is going to look at all the pictures of your wedding for the next few decades or more, so you need to like it.

Don't just pick the first dress you try on – unless you try on more and go back to that dress and still feel it is the "one."

You have several major decisions to make prior to choosing your new fairy-tale gown.

Do you already have a venue in mind for the ceremony or reception? If so, the venue and the gown need to flow seamlessly together.

But please note! I did not say that if you're going to the beach or Vegas you cannot wear a ball gown, or if you are in your local church you cannot wear a strapless mermaid. It really isn't about all that (unless your church has rules about it).

Some brides get so neurotic trying to seem educated on all the terms when they walk into the local bridal boutique, they usually throw around lingo they believe the sales consultant will understand – and more than half of them don't.

For instance, silhouettes for bridal gowns have been blended through new and creative designers in the market. An A-line is rarely a simple A-line and a ball gown doesn't necessarily mean a huge poof-ball like it used to.

Don't get stuck on terms.

Half the people out there cannot tell you the difference between a mermaid and a trumpet and almost anything that is in the fit-and-flair category is being called mermaid – although it's not – but whatever. In my opinion, empire (if you want to get technical, pronounced am-pee-err) waist dresses are meant for people that are toothpick size or pregnant. That isn't what the encyclopedia says, but that's what FairyBridemother says. So, if you have a lot of curves, go for a drop waist or mermaid to show them off. Soapbox over.

So...... whether you get a sheath, A-line, empire, drop waist, fit-and-flair, ball gown, mermaid, trumpet, long line, basque waist, fitted, flowy, plain, embellished, simple or over-the-top gown, just focus on feeling and looking amazing!

Remember the goal is to look and FEEL like a million dollars, and if a gown doesn't make you *feel* and *think* the best about your body, it probably isn't your gown.

Now, please don't think I mean that you have to have some major emotional experience in your gown when you try it on at the store. It doesn't always happen and certain reality shows have made it appear that unless everyone around you and you are weeping uncontrollably, having a meltdown, and screwing up your makeup, it isn't the gown....

Well, that just isn't the case.

But you should feel amazing regardless of all the weepy stuff.

Purchase one of those big wedding magazines that have 350 gowns on display. Make sure you like the selection, tear out the pages spanning a wide array of styles you like then ask your groom to look at the pages of gowns from the magazine and take note of his reaction to them, and make notes! (Are you seeing a theme here?) If he goes ga-ga over something, make sure you at least try on a gown like it to see if you like it too.

Don't be offended if your groom doesn't want you to remind him of his grandmother's tablecloth when he sees a few lace dresses. It is easier to go shopping for your favorite gown that will suit you, if you have this guidance from your groom. You can still surprise him with all your glorious gorgeousness even if he has seen a picture of "the" gown. He won't remember it was one he picked out unless you tell him later.

Remember, you are only getting his input so you don't try on and fall in love with something he's going to poke fun of that day or in later years when you look through your wedding album.

Categorize these photos by style and also be armed with pictures of gowns you have seen on the magical virtual pinboard that no one can ever find where to purchase....

We are a very visually stimulated society.

That said take a few tear outs or printed out photos of gowns with which you really resonate to show your gown consultant and be prepared to tell her the ultimate information – why! Tell her *how* you want to *feel* and *what* you're trying to accomplish within the overall scope of your big day.

Fact

Only 60% of brides find their perfect gown on their first outing. You may be the 40% that just need a little more time.

Every time you try on a gown, try to be detailed about the parts you like and do not care for at all. Finally, remain calm. The goal is to look and feel stunning. Try not to get too focused in on a specific dress you've only seen online or in a magazine – that dress may look very different in person or on your body than in that picture.

Remember that you may change your mind on the style of gown you like and are drawn to during the flow of trying on these amazing creations. ***Speak up!*** Let the consultant know that you would like to venture into a different style that may better suit your body or your tastes. To make sure you use your time wisely, tell her specifically what you like and don't like about every dress and allow her to make suggestions.

Have all your pictures with you to remind yourself what your soon-to-be husband may poke fun at and avoid venturing there. That would be tragic to show up in a gown that he described as "it looks like a bird exploded on it." Don't even try on these sorts of gowns.

Also remember that there are tons of accessories to consider such as veil, headband or tiara, crinoline to support the skirt, special corset bra for posture (so none of your pictures will show you slumping or pooching), shoes, if you are wearing stockings, etc. that complete your ensemble. Remember these items when conveying the budget for your gown – because they will most likely max your budget with the gown and then add on those items afterward.

Be very open with your consultant about your **time frame**, **price tag limits**, and about all the information you have spent time developing because they know the inventory of their store better than you and there could be an amazing treasure lurking on the back rack she may think of for you.

No Pressure.....But......

Just keep in mind that you really cannot proceed with the balance of your wedding planning until after you have purchased your gown. Do NOT be tempted to force your way through the other steps until you have found your gown.

Remember, I already said this in this chapter, but it bears repeating until it is done. Your gown and venues set the tone for everything else in your wedding. They are what will guide you through the execution of your theme.

This is not an item to let wait.

Now, go have fun in Barbie Bridal Zone!

Try on everything you thought you would say "no" to – including veils and tiaras!

Accessorize! Stylize!

Play!

Then prioritize before making that final purchase.

Get it done and be happy with your choice once it is made!

Questions:

Can I take my gown home today? (most gowns are made by machines and there can be up to a one inch variance in each dress of the same size – if this one fits perfectly, the next one may need alterations)

If I have to order, how long will it take to receive my gown once it is ordered? (make sure to use the last possible date it could arrive and make sure it fits within your time frame of tentative dates you have already discussed with your groom – don't get anxious)

How long will it take to make alterations to my gown?

When can we begin selecting the Bridesmaid dresses?

How long will they typically take to arrive?

How long will they take to be altered?

What is the latest possible date that all this will be completed?

The answers to these questions will help you understand whether your tentative dates are going to work out for you.

If your dates will work, make the purchase, set a date for your bridesmaids to choose their dresses in a timely fashion, and proceed immediately to shopping for a ceremony and reception venue(s).

If your dates will not work with how long it will take to receive and alter your gown, **is your date flexible? If not,** ask if there is a rush fee you can pay to get it here in time, or choose another gown that will fit within your timeframe.

If so, order your gown. Go back to your groom, parents, and his parents and see what new tentative dates after the gown will arrive. Once you have targeted new dates that will work, shop for venues.

Remember to complete this task before moving on, no matter how you are tempted!!!!

Headpieces & Veils

After selecting your gown, remember most of your photos are waist/chest up memorializing your big day. No wedding day ensemble is complete without something special in your hair – whether it is a sparkly comb, headband, little spirals, a tiara or veil.

It is best to select these items while in your gown even if you don't do it the same day as your gown selection. Have a general idea of wearing your hair up or down nomatter the style and choose your headpieces accordingly.

As for veils, there are many styles from which to choose.

I personally love the longer flowing sort called fingertip or walking veils. Cathedral veils give an even more dramatic yet softer look, but every veil does not go with every gown and there is no rule of thumb, so to speak. You simply need to try some on and see what works best for you personally.

I need to address a few personal pet peeves about veils with you. If you purchase a single-layer veil, it only goes on the back of your head. Do not have a single-layer veil and flip it over your face leaving the back of your head exposed for your walk down the aisle. Also, if your veil is two-layer, typically there is beading or edging of some sort on the edge and if you flip that first layer over in front of your face, the beading will be backward and no longer sparkle or make sense visually – it can also cause a harsh line in your photos.

If you want a piece over your face for the father to push back when he kisses you on the cheek while giving you away, or fiancé to push back when the officiant says "you may now kiss your bride" either purchase a separate "blusher" or purchase a veil that already come with a blusher layer that has no trim around the edge. Having a trim around the edge of a blusher will simply break the fluid look of your gown with a line or design and visually cuts your look in half.

A raw edge blusher is the best way to go so there is only a beautiful picture of you while you're walking down the aisle and nothing to distract from your beauty and your beautiful gown selection.

Keep your theme in mind while completing your look, but also how your headpiece makes you feel. Stoic brides have melted in tears after seeing a veil on their head. It can truly complete your look and your personal emotional experience as well.

So, Congratulations Sweet Bride-to-Be!

Now that the gown is in the bag,
we can move on to the next step which is **venues**.

However, do a brief check and see exactly what your funds look like prior to shopping for venues.

You never want to waste time or energy by shopping outside your price range. It's a waste of time, emotional energy, and peace of mind.

If you do not feel as though you have sufficient funds, see if you need to negotiate some funds from others or other areas because you went overboard for your dress, or if you found a major deal on your gown, you may have more to spare for other items that are important to you.

Either way, make sure you know what you are shopping *with* before you go shopping! There is no time to dawdle or window shop, so to speak.

VENUE SELECTION

So, here we are at the place doves will fly and butterflies will dance, and all your sweet love for each other will be made public. Now whether you did this part before or after the gown, it is still in the top 2 in a long, long list of decisions for your big day!

Remember: The ambiance that your venue already provides will dictate how much money you will need to spend on décor to simply enhance or to entirely cover up any undesirable things.

The dress, the venue, and the food are the most important decisions for enjoyment, AND they are also the largest chunk of your budget. This is why we are getting these items done first. You will know exactly where you stand with the balance of your budget to pay for everything else your big day requires to be beautiful and well documented.

Prior to calling any venue, have several dates that you and your families have discussed as possible wedding dates.

Remember: Don't just go straight to the price. Find out what is included with each facility. Sometimes, you have a venue that is very inexpensive, however, you have to purchase or rent everything from an outside source that can throw you way over your intended budget.

For instance, some resorts may seem high initially; however, they include everything including the cake and sometimes an overnight stay for you and your hubby the night after. Take everything into consideration before ruling out a venue.

Your venue and catering are going to eat up about half of your total budget – or more.

Ceremony:
Church Wedding:

The most popular still is a church, synagogue or worship center wedding. Even if some people do not attend church or believe in God, some just really want their weddings inside a church.

Whether it is for the architectural details that show up in photographs, or if it is the love of your worship center and God that draws you to this idea, there is a vast array of worship centers to choose from. However, you need to keep in mind that every denomination and religion has their own guidelines and you may need to call quite a few in order to find one that will fit your needs.

Begin with your personal place of worship, parent's worship center, or the buildings you are most aesthetically drawn toward. Make a list of all that you would initially consider.

The list of questions for finding this category of venue is quite different than for any other ceremonial venue. The main thing is not to get discouraged if your first few choices don't work out. You didn't find your man overnight either.

Do take note of this one thing, the likelihood of you booking a Catholic church without being Catholic will probably be impossible. Many worship centers will not permit people who are not members of their own congregation, denomination, or parish to use their facilities for wedding ceremonies. Some will allow the use, but it is a different pricing structure than if you were a member. You may be required to attend their proprietary premarital counseling course(s) and use their approved officiant.

Remember, within the worship community, marriage is not just a piece of legal documentation; it is a holy sacrament. But the benefits of church weddings can also outweigh the hoops that you may need to jump through to have one.

If you ever had the idea that you might attend or join a congregation after your wild single days were over and settle down into a family lifestyle, the place where you get married may be a great way to start down that path. You will already have built-in supporters for your married life and any bumps in the marriage road can be addressed with the same minister that already knows you and possibly even marries the two of you.

The counseling that some churches require can help you to see potential arguments before they begin and open a non-confrontational avenue to address your individual ideals as well as discover and validate those you may agree on as a couple. The process can strengthen your relationship and truly prepare you for what marriage holds. So don't be afraid when this subject is addressed while speaking to any worship center about what you may have to "endure" to hold your wedding ceremony in their facility.

When calling:

May I speak to the minister or coordinator that handles weddings?

Do you have a handbook that I could review to see if we qualify to have our wedding at your facility? *Many times approaching the director in this way will allow them to help you negotiate the maze of requirements.*

I worship somewhere else, but I love your facility. May I have my minister perform our ceremony? Do I need to be aware of any restrictions?

What facilities are available for my bridal party to dress?

Do we need to arrive completely dressed for the ceremony? If so, is there a room I am able to hide for last minute preparations before the walk down the aisle?

Is there a designated wedding coordinator?

Is there a night to do a rehearsal with the wedding coordinator?

Is there any décor already on-site and available to be used for my ceremony? Is there any décor that is prohibited by your policies? *Be sure to address the policies prior to planning any décor to ensure you are in compliance with that facility's policy.*

Are there any other events going on that day?

Would I also be able to use the on-site fellowship hall or dining room for my reception? And if so, what are the restrictions on dance, décor, music, food, or alcohol?

What are the time constraints for everything we have discussed?

Are we required to have live music, or can we use a soundtrack?

Will we have access to the sound system?

Do you have an approved list of music?

Do you have an approved list of musicians or vocalists for the wedding?

Is there handicap access?

What costs should I expect to pay for the use of the sanctuary, fellowship hall, minister, coordinator, rehearsal, music, sound coordinator, and/or counseling?

Non-Church Wedding:

There is a growing array of ceremony sites available to exchange your wedding vows. Theme Parks, State Parks, Beaches, Hotels, Restaurants, Resorts, Country Clubs, Convention Centers, Courthouses, Museums, Vegas Chapels, and Cruise Ships. The list is endless and can be a bit daunting. But THIS is why we did some research into what we have been dreaming about already, right?

Now, we can eliminate a lot of these options based on the following:

Does it work with my theme that is beginning to take shape? *(because I already did my homework on developing my style, and I already purchased my gown)*

Is my dress too much or not enough for this particular venue *(and by this, we mean YOUR idea of too much or not enough – no one else's idea of either, remember that! – do they flow together or can you MAKE them flow together? If you want to wear a ball gown on a beach, you go right ahead! Just bring some bling with you to the sandy altar of love.)*

If you always dreamed of an outdoor wedding, well that narrows down a few places. Focus on those venues.

Remember that if you go to a park or beach, call the related county and ask them if you need a permit and find out all the details on how to apply, how much the permit is, how long it will take to get the permit, and the restrictions for using the location.

No matter the venue you phone, ask the following questions:

Is my date available?

Is there handicap access?

Is there space for me and my party to get ready on-site or do we need to arrive dressed and ready to go?

Are tables and chairs already on-site? If I need to rent tables, chairs, etc., what companies have you worked with in the past that I could rely on to set up my wedding here?

Is there a sound system for music or musicians? or Do we need to bring a sound system? Is there access to electrical outlets?

Who would be available to receive floral and rental deliveries on my behalf?

Is there a day-of coordinator?

When could we book a rehearsal?

What décor is provided, allowed, or prohibited?

How much time will be allotted for the setup and breakdown of my ceremonial items?

Will your staff setup and/or breakdown my decoration items?

Reception:

Is the reception being held at the same venue as the ceremony?

If not, is the facility available on the date I would like to have my wedding?

Ask if there are any other events or weddings booked for that day. And if so, does that inflict any time constraints on you and your party?

If you are flexible with your time table as well as your day or date, you may ask for a better rate when the subject of money becomes the topic of discussion. Now is not the time to bring this up. Find out all the information you need to know to make a solid decision prior to discussing money.

You should already have an idea of how much a venue charges in general by looking at their website prior to ever contacting them directly. If they do not list packages and prices on their website, have a friend or parent call and ask for the information.

What is the color scheme of the room we would be using?

May I see pictures of other weddings and receptions in this room?

What decorations do you provide?

Are there any restrictions on providing my own decorations?

Are there any decorations that are not permitted?

Will our guests have to pay to park?

Do I need to hire a parking attendant or valet?

Are there any events scheduled that will make parking difficult for my guest?

What's the maximum number of guests you can accommodate?

Are there coat racks for our guests?

Is a sound system available?

Will we need to bring in sound equipment?

Are there any areas we won't have access to?

Are the facility and bathrooms handicapped accessible?

May I choose my own vendors or is there an in-house service or list I have to choose from?

How many hours do you allow a party to be here?

Is there set-up time and break-down time already in the timeframe or is that additional?

Does this facility have air conditioning or heat in every room?

What's the site fee? And what does that include?

Is there a day-of coordinator? Is she an additional charge?

Do you provide cake services?

Is there an on-site cake-cutting fee for an outside vendor's cake?

Can we bring in our own booze? Is there a "corkage" fee, and do we need a license?

Are favors allowed if they contain alcohol?

If the venue is a community center or historic venue: Would I need to rent chairs and tables or are they provided?

If the venue is a hotel: What room rate can you offer our guests? And how many rooms can you guarantee us at that rate?

Visit the facility prior to giving a deposit. On the tour, ask:

Where will you put the band, dance floor, cake table, gift table, coffee service?

Are there different sized dance floors? Is there an additional charge to use them or could we just designate a carpeted area for dancing? *(only consider a carpeted area if money is a real obstacle or your guests just really aren't the dancing kind)*

Make a comment about any existing decorations you see and like or don't like. Ask "Will this still be available on my wedding date?" Or "Does this have to be here or could it be moved?"

Where is the best place to make our grand entrance the night of the reception?

Where can my party and I hide, if needed, until the reception starts and we make our grand entrance? May I use this room to change clothes or freshen up during the reception?

Ask if you may have a drawing of the room!!! Get a blank one as well as one where you and the person giving your tour draw where everything will go. Put a copy with the contract, and keep a copy for yourself.

This will help you visualize everywhere your decorations will be and envision the flow of the evening. If you see a snag in how the room is set up, make sure to give a new drawing of the layout you want to the coordinator with your dated signature. Keep a copy.

If the venue offers only in-house catering, be sure to address all the questions in the "Foodies" section prior to getting a complete quote.

After receiving a tour, addressing all your concerns including lighting *(see below)*, and if the venue measures up to what you had hoped, ask "Does anything we've seen today cost extra or is everything I see included in the price you quoted?"

Ask to quote you with and without a cocktail hour *(see below if you would like to include this event to fill time between the ceremony and reception)* if you are feeling like the figure is going to be too high. Also ask what is making the dollar figure higher? I am looking for where I can make a few cuts and get closer to the figure I had in mind.

Ask for their deposit and cancellation policy.

Hopefully, you won't have to worry about cancelling but it is always best to know everything in advance of making a legal commitment.

Cocktail hour

Cocktail hour has been a growing trend for the past few decades. What is it, you ask? It is an event that eats up some time and provides some refreshment and even entertainment for your guests while they wait between the ceremony and the reception. In some circles, it is a MUST.

If you plan to have a cocktail hour, here are some items to plan to make it a successful one:

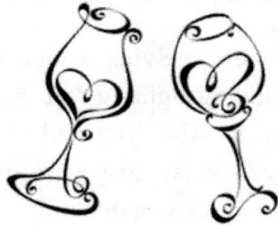

If you have decided to implement a cocktail hour, inform your guests on the programs they received at your ceremony. It is always more comfortable for guests to be informed of "what's next?" even if it is only in general. If you have an elaborate affair and someone notable is singing, performing, or entertaining during this segment, mention that as well on the program to create momentum for the performer as well as the guests. This will have your guests looking forward to the lag between the ceremony and reception.

What lighter food would provide some distraction for your guests? What would flow with your theme? What would be different and make people talk, crack jokes, and smile? If you are doing something completely zany, be sure to mention it on the back of the program – unless it is a surprise, that is.

Where will you house the cocktail hour? It should not be in the same area/room as your reception. Does this area have enough capacity for all the people attending your wedding? Is there an opportunity for recorded music to be played or do you need to schedule or hire a musician(s) for this part of the day?

Usually, you do not need to worry about seating at a cocktail hour, however, if you plan to have a few older guests, consider having chairs there specifically for them and consider putting their names on their chairs. This will make them feel cared for as well as deter any criticism for not having seating for everyone.

Now, side note, if your cocktail hour is going to be a bit longer, on pavement, not have entertainment or games of some kind to keep people moving about, you may want to consider the option of chairs and even tables. A few high-top tables are always a good option regardless of your choosing chairs or no chairs. This gives people an opportunity to stop the balancing act between their plate and drink and avoid Uncle Roy from having a big red splotch on his white tuxedo.

Lighting

Lighting is absolutely crucial for the success of your event. You may want a warmly and dimly lit room, but what if your guests cannot see their food to eat? Remember to speak to your venue about lighting options for the reception and find out their recommendations as well as if you are able to have burning candles on the tables.

Some venues will only permit battery operated candles, so you need to be prepared to have several different sources of light for your event. The best blends are layering low house lights, tall candelabras, and votive candles on the tables surrounding the centerpieces, along with various spotlights around the room targeting photo ops, the cake, the dance floor, and food and drink stations.

IF

If your reception venue does not include catering, move on to the list of caterers you were provided by your potential venue and ask the questions from the Foodies section of the book prior to booking the venue. If there is no approved list, and you're trying to keep cost low, call Aunt Addie and ask for her famous jambalaya.

After deciding exactly how much you can afford to spend on your reception, subtract 5% for any last minute potential expenses, then factor how many guests you will be able to accommodate within that dollar figure.

Stick to your guns on this number of guests so it will make it easier and understandable for the person requesting to bring a last minute addition. Also, you have padded yourself for just such an occasion that you can at-will add a last-minute person that you really wanted to be there in the first place.

Repeat this process with as many venues as needed in order to land at the right look at the right price accommodating the most number of people.

Are you booked?

Congratulations!

Now, take pictures of everything in that venue you need to remember for the balance of your planning, along with pictures of the plated food items that you agreed to serve as well, and put those photos in your style guide.

Next:

Is your wedding six or more months away?

Do you plan to invite out-of town guests?

If you answer "yes" to either of these questions, send out save-the-date cards to the out-of-towners, family, planned attendants, and any people you cannot live without being present at your wedding, but only to them.

#1 You will get a head start on your address list for invitations

#2 You will know very quickly whether these people absolutely can or cannot make your event.

Make sure these save-the-cards are mailed between six and nine months prior to your wedding. They should include the date, city, and state or foreign destination for your celebration.

Next:

Firm up your list of attendants.

How many attendants will the ceremony facility allow you to have?

Now, ask the ones who haven't been properly invited or just make the ask official. Make sure your groom has his list and that you coordinate this for both sides of the aisle.

Try to have the same number of bridesmaids as groomsmen, but do not stress if you are one off. As a solution, one can always escort two from the other side just so long as that one isn't you or your groom, that is.

By all means, don't just get another person on either side just for visually balance things out. Remember, these people are supposed to be trusted and committed to your vision. If they aren't or can't be that, you don't want them helping you plan or sabotage your day.

Next:

Now that the venue is booked and you know exactly how many people will be able to host at your wedding, and you know who of your save-the-date people can make your celebration, start your guest list wars. I say that in a joking manner. Remember, we are avoiding drama......

If the number is small, keep it to adults only, and avoid too many "plus 1"s for your single friends. Of course, make allowances for your attendants and close family who have a serious relationship to invite their significant other.

Make sure to immediately add the people who will be helping you the day of your wedding outside of your wedding party. Usually, they will not need to bring a "plus 1", but let it naturally come up in conversation while they are helping you work toward your goals as to whether you should extend the offer.

You may find that your list can fill up very quickly, so don't be quick about telling everyone *where* and *when* because you could find some uninvited guests at your small event.

FOODIES

The food is probably the most forgettable thing about a wedding for your guests – unless it is over-the-top amazing or bad.

It is very important for your food to taste good!
And that there is enough of it!

I know that sounds elementary and like it should be a given, however, you would be surprised at the limited, amazingly mediocre fair that has been served at such a special occasion.

Make certain to get a sample of the foodies your caterer intends to serve!

Remember, the food is for your guests. You will probably never have time or the settled nerves to eat during your reception. It will be a blur. So, here is a list to get you started on what to serve.

Are there special foods from your families' histories that should be represented? By this, I mean, will there be a large number of your guests that will be very disappointed if there isn't some representation of your family heritage.

Are there foods that are strictly prohibited by the religion of the majority of your guests?

For instance, if there will be a large number of Jewish or Islamic people, you may want to forget about having the bacon bar. If there will be a large number of Hindu people, forget the beef stroganoff, etc. You get the point. If half your family is allergic to shellfish, avoid the lobster selection.

Only you, your groom, and your caterer will probably be making these selections, so make certain you have covered this item with respective family members from both sides prior to setting your menu for the big party.

If there is a way to weave your magic theme through a menu item or two, that would be the ultimate choice.

The kind of food that you choose to serve will depend on what kind of budget you are looking at as well as what theme you have chosen for your event. You may opt for barbeque chicken with corn on the cob, steak and potatoes, sushi with hibachi-grilled shrimp, or tapas and paella. Of course, that doesn't mean if you are planning on peacock theme to serve pheasant. That might gross a few people out.

Remember that if you are allowing children at your wedding, discuss having a less-expensive, kid-friendly option for them. (and make sure your venue has an out of the way place in the room for them to congregate and play where their parents can see them but still enjoy their evening celebrating you)

The timing of how the food comes out is something you can request of your caterer. You can set designated cues within the reception to begin serving certain items, or you can have all your food served back to back and leave it to the discretion of the table servers. You could also have salads or appetizers already on the table just as soon as your guests enter the ballroom just to curb any hunger complaints. But if you have had a cocktail hour with food this won't be necessary.

Alcohol

First question on this subject is do you want to offer alcohol at your reception?

Second, will your venue choice allow alcohol to be on the premises?

If yes, will they allow alcohol to be brought in by you, or do you have to purchase it through the venue?

Do they provide the bartenders or are you allowed to have your own provided?

This is all covered in the venue section, however, this part bears repeating because alcohol can be a very controversial subject for different religions, cultures, and some venues can suffer legal ramifications for not having proper insurance or licensing for serving or selling alcoholic products.

Specialty drink

With today's budgetary constraints, some couples have opted for serving one or two specialty drinks instead of having an open bar – in general or at cocktail hour.

Of course, you will need to check with your venue and/or caterer to make sure you can take advantage of this option, or have them create a cocktail specifically to represent your day.

Having glasses filled with unusual colors that flow from your theme will be the talk of the party – especially if the drink options taste as good as they look. It is a fun way to great your guests while they try to find things to talk about.

This can be a nice addition to the standard drinks that are traditionally offered in catering packages such as water, coffee, and iced tea.

Cake

Your wedding cake is probably the single most expensive piece of combined food and artwork that was ever invented. Yet, despite their usual beauty on the outside, they do not always taste as marvelous as they look which is sad considering. Be sure to get a tasting from your baker prior to penning the check to purchase this artistic creation.

Buffet or Sit Down

Remember, this is mostly going to be discussed with

your caterer, however, let's talk about the upsides and downsides to each of these options.

This one decision sets the tone for your entire reception, so let's dive into the options and what they bring to the table for you.

Buffet dinners can feel less formal. You must decide if you will allow people to serve themselves or have servers tend each buffet tray and dip the foodies out for the guests which would ensure that each guest has the opportunity to taste everything.

If you allow people to serve themselves, you could easily run out of food before everyone is fed because some people do not understand the word "moderation." Feeding people is typically the primary chunk of your budget, so it is important that your dollar stretches over all your invited guests and no one is left hungry.

Also, make certain to have a label on or in front of each food tray that has the title of the dish and if it is exotic, make sure to have a brief list of its contents to avoid any allergy problems for your guests.

A sit-down or plated dinner usually produces a more formal and possibly pampered feel. Guests are seated when they are served by hired wait staff. This option is usually the more expensive of the two, but this is not the area to skimp if you are envisioning a super glamorous, formal, and/or elegant evening affair. You should be prepared for providing an appetizer, salad or soup, and main course at a minimum.

Usually, you will need to allow guests to choose between meats or a vegetarian or kosher option on the RSVP.

This option does come with a bit more demand for planning, money, and attention to detail. However, the results can bless your guests with an amazing sense of well-being when they leave your affair.

Questions

Here is a list of quality questions to ask each caterer. You will find that you come up with questions of your own. Add them to the list as you think of them to remember to ask the next caterer that you interview.

Take a lot of notes. Make certain you have covered every topic that is important to you and that you have received satisfactory answers. These notes will help ensure that all the important items are listed out in the contract, and you can make a solid list for your catering manager and day-of coordinator to follow.

If the caterer is in-house to the venue, you will want to ask most these questions prior to booking your venue.

This list is meant to be step-by-step for an outside caterer, even if this caterer was recommended by your venue.

I have booked (reception venue) for (date and time). Are you available to cater my wedding reception?

I'm having a (theme) wedding. What are your most popular dishes that would complement my theme?

Are your menus set, or do I have some flexibility with mixing and matching what I want? May I customize the menu by requesting that you use a family recipe?

Are you able to accommodate dietary restrictions if guests have any?

If I have a list of certain foods I absolutely don't want, will your kitchen comply?

Will you provide a tasting so I may try some options for each course of the meal? (*cake, wine and champagne*) (*anything they are providing in the contract*)

May I see photos of the dishes you prepare?

May I see photos of the way the servers are dressed that will be serving at my event? (*if super themed, ask if you provide costumes or accessories, will the servers wear them during the event?*)

May I review your standard contract?

What deposit is required to hold my desired date?

Under what terms is my deposit refundable?

If I provide my wedding cake from an outside vendor, am I charged an additional fee for cutting and serving the cake?

Do you or will you have any other events or weddings the same day or weekend as my wedding?

Do you provide a children's meal? *(if so is there a reduced per child cost?)*

Do you provide a less expensive meal option for my vendors, such as the band, DJ, photographers and videographers?

Do you have a liquor license, and, if so, do you provide brand-name liquors? May I purchase my own? Is there a corkage fee for bringing your own wine or champagne? If so, how much is the fee?

Will you provide a bartender? If so, what are the charges?

What does your insurance cover?

Based on our conversation details, will you offer a final per-person estimate? (make sure you have discussed a tentative number of guests) If this figure is out of your budget, ask them where we could trim the costs without suffering the menu?

Is sales tax included in the contract?

Does this cost cover just the food, or does it include linens, utensils, dishes and glassware usage as well?

Will this cost include the service staff, gratuities, and cleanup?

Is there an increase or decrease in the per-person cost if my number of guests goes above or below a certain number? For instance, if I trim my list to 50 or include everyone and invite 200 guests?

Will a catering manager be on site during the reception to overcome any problems? If so, do they you an additional fee for that service?

Is there an additional fee for staff overtime?

What are the shapes of the tables, and how many people can sit comfortably at each?

What's the ratio of servers to guests?

What are the terms for paying on this contract after the initial deposit?

Wedding Insurance

If any party of your wedding day is staged outside without a plan B option, you may want to look into some wedding insurance. Wedding insurance will cover a myriad of losses, but the main one is if you had to reschedule your entire event due to catastrophic weather.

Quite frankly, even if you are just having an expensive affair, there are all sorts of other items wedding insurance will cover including vendors that go bankrupt after you have paid for their services and you will not get the services for which you paid. It can be an invaluable tool to circumvent disaster.

Wedding insurance is not for everyone, but many can benefit from it, so make certain to check it out for yourself and see if it is a potential fit to help protect your plans.

ATTENDANTS

This is a very important topic that goes right along with the section on building your team. Who do you officially ask to stand up with you for your vows? Best friends, close friends, or people you have been friends with on/off throughout your entire life are usually the quickest choices. However, some people are also thrust upon you from the other side of this union, like the groom's sister that absolutely hates you.

The best choices are usually the go-getter get-er-done girls that are committed to your vision of your big day. The girls, who will defend your choices to others, be on your side, and able to put in some time with you to help you put things together are the only girls you want to involve this closely in your planning.

This section is to help you navigate your way through the final choices as well as understanding what their roles are supposed to be and if they are capable of fulfilling those roles. So here we go.

When wedding parties get too large, all sorts of drama can ensue. However, if you manage wisely, you can have people invested in your vision and coming together to make your wedding dreams come true.

Who are the people you just cannot imagine having your wedding without – outside of your betrothed. (favorite sister, bestie, cousin, etc.) Make a list right now of those people.

Add on for a few that have already sort-of invited themselves into your party, and then add on for the one or two from the groom's side that has sort of been invited already by someone other than yourself.

Is the list too long? Only you and your groom can answer that question. If you now have 10 people on that list and your groom, who is an introvert, only intends to have three of his inner circle stand up for him, you must whittle your list down to your most important people.

But say you are the one who doesn't have a lot of super-close friends and he is the life of the party and all his frat buddies want to be involved, again, a negotiation must take place.

Now, your number does not have to be exactly the same on each side. You may have more than one escort for one of the bridesmaids or groomsmen – just don't get too lopsided. There are many creative ways to allow others to be part of your big day without them standing on the stage or the expense on their part of a new tux, tux rental, or a $200 dress.

Consider having designated ushers or usher-istas for the overflow of attendants on either side. They can still dress up, care for the moms, and usher the guests and still be very involved.

Have them greet your guests and ensure they sign the guest book or art or whatever method you choose. Equip them with information to pass along to guests from what to do with presents brought to the ceremony down to spare maps to the reception. Have them greet people at the reception and direct traffic there.

These designations should be for your loved ones that want to help you in some way but are unable to help you actually plan out or execute your wedding plans, maybe they are from out of town but they want to be a part of your day.

The trick is you need volunteers. When someone offers to do something for you for your wedding and they have not been asked to be a bridesmaid or groomsman – either due to size of the party, you're not having attendants, or you had not considered including them before (mainly because you cannot think of everyone and everything), you are then poised with roles and functions for people to fill immediately without any embarrassment on either person's part.

Who are your parents trying to get you to put in the wedding party?

Who are your best friends of all time?

Who are the most helpful?

Who have your best interest in mind and can make things about "you" and not themselves?

Who is responsible?

Who is the most organized?

Who would be absolutely crushed or devastated not to be in or a part of your wedding?

Do you still have too many people to choose from?

Eliminate anyone who has a hard time keeping any secrets. Your bridesmaids and other fairy helpers will be all up in your business and personal thoughts, fears, and you want them, nay need them, to cheer with you when milestones are achieved.

Eliminate anyone who is going to be under serious financial stress trying to do everything that is necessary to support you. Remember there can be travel expenses, dresses, shoes, beauty services, gifts, hosting the shower, and more. Make sure someone close is still involved or has a role but just not necessarily that of a bridesmaid.

Eliminate anyone who simply cannot or will not participate or help you (or the team) to research, execute or complete anything toward your goals. This is a working role that needs active and excited participants to make things happen.

Now that you have your list honed down to what you feel is a reasonable number, and your groom has close to the same number to offset the sides - it is time to get down to some serious planning with your girls.

It is time to set the standard for what you truly expect of your attendants. They need guidance, BUT, keep it realistic. Remember that you are the one getting married which means *you* will be doing most of the work.

The Bridesmaids are your *helpers*. They are there to *help* you execute the decisions you have made. They need to get along with each other and work together as a team to make it happen without a lot of drama.

Keep in constant contact, but keep the communication flowing both ways.

Consider hosting a Bridesmaid lunch or dinner meeting.
(hosting means you pay for this get together)

First, you want to thank them in advance for putting up with you, working hard, and helping your achieve your dream wedding.

Second, you want to go over your vision and set the stage for everything you would like to achieve.

Third, you should present information below in some written form to them so everyone can buy in to your expectations. You may want to add some specific things to your list that are not covered below. The following is just to get you started. Ask for volunteers for these different tasks and write their names on your copy for those tasks. This will help you keep track of who offered what to help you.

Fourth, set a date for shopping for dresses, accessories, etc. Agree not to exceed a certain dollar figure for their attire so they can begin planning for that expenditure.

Fifth, set dates for the bridal shower and bachelorette party as well as rehearsal and wedding date if already known.

Sixth, you may want to reveal a sample of any items you have already purchased or your vision board as visual aids for your girls to get the energy flowing, and ideas popping on how to achieve these things without breaking your budget.

Of course, these are in addition to expected items like:

Addressing invitations

Keeping track of responses

Keeping track of gifts from showers

Addressing thank you notes

Making decorations

Making favors

Organizing showers

Helping the Maid of Honor with the bachelorette party

Purchasing the dress the bride selects for the wedding

Note: you need to select their dress! They are looking for guidance from you and a good bridesmaid will wear whatever you pick out for her. Just use discretion in your choice so they don't look like cupcakes or slutty.

Attend the wedding. (sounds a little obvious, but is your wedding date achievable on their existing calendar?)

Participate in as many activities as you are able. Please make these dates a priority. Let the Maid of Honor know if you are already planning to be out of town or have scheduled other commitments right away. (The Maid of Honor should have a calendar of all schedules and scheduled events with who is and isn't available at all times.)

Here are a few things to add to your list that most people don't think of to ask and some bridesmaids would never think to offer:

Assemble an emergency kit for the day of the wedding.

Make sure I eat something substantial during the day of the wedding.

Make sure I drink a lot of water.

Keep tissue on hand.

Smile! A lot! Sometimes smiling can put me at ease and help affirm me in the choices I have made.

Put together a checklist of the items I want to keep from the ceremony and reception (and get one of the programs, favors, some of the flowers or a centerpiece, etc.

for when I return from the honeymoon)

Go check on how the ceremony décor looks, how many people have arrived, if the right music is playing, etc.

Help me make returns on unused items after the wedding.

When you have a free moment, ask me what I left to do, but only accept a task if you can help.

The day of the wedding, if I am unaware that something is wrong and it is being fixed or handled, please don't tell me – unless of course it is a real emergency – use your best judgment. You know me, remember?!

Help me pack for the honeymoon and make sure I have my travel information and such altogether.

Make sure I choose and lay out work outfits for the following week for my return so I look fresh and together for my return to work.

I will try to get as much input as I can on the Bridesmaid dress, but once the decision is made, please don't tell me you hate it.

Let me know when you've accomplished something for me.

Please get along with each other.

When I ask for something, please respond as soon as possible – even if you have to tell me you can talk about it later in the day or next week. It may be time-sensitive and I can always delegate it to someone else if you won't be available.

DÉCOR

Décor is by far my favorite part of any major or even small event. Décor creates the ambiance, sets the tone and feel for the special occasion. Of course, I just think of magical things and wave my magic wand and "poof" they're done. But I recognize you have to do it the harder way. But that doesn't mean it has to be "hard" or "not fun." Quite the opposite indeed.

When selecting the items in "your style," what are the most important items to you?

Remember that more pictures will be taken in one spot in the ceremony, the altar. So make the altar pop even if you have to let the other décor slide a little for the ceremony.

For the reception, people mill around quite a bit. It is better to have several main focal points in the room than to spend time and money on a lot of little items that do not make a grand statement and will never be photographed or remembered. Focus your time, energy and dollars where it counts!

Here is the first thing to consider – COLOR

What do you already have to work with or work around?

What is the color of the ceremony venue?

What is the color of the reception venue?

In what colors are the Bridesmaids dresses available?

Whether you like it or not, the venues' color schemes matter because no matter how hard you try to overcome them, if you pick a color that clashes, it will show and feel "off" somehow which will affect your overall happiness.

So here is the trick. You have your venue colors, you have your style guide for the look you are trying to achieve, and undoubtedly you have your and your groom's favorite colors and seasons with which to contend. Now, it is time to use your good taste and your dream team's good taste to finalize the color scheme.

Once it is set. There is no looking back.

Get swatches of all the colors – give each Dream Team décor member a swatch tassel. (just staple all the fabrics together that make up the pallet – you can make this pretty by wrapping a cord or ribbon around the top where it is stapled)

Dream Team assignments:

Shop for items online and locally to use to create the visions the bride has provided

Report how much things are and in what quantity you get a price break (you may be able to use the same thing in several different ways and even make a real statement if you have enough of one thing).

Make sure to send a link if online, photo of item, and pricing info in one message for each item. This will keep everything from being confusing for your bride and for you.

Now, if you collectively think something elaborate can be made, discuss it with the bride and key members of the dream team – only recruit outside help if the bride approves because some things may be secret. Let the bride know how much in total you can make "x" item for and after gaining approval, proceed.

Invitations

Now, it is time to shop for wedding invitations or start designing your own. Be sure that if you make your own wedding invitations that you are getting a superior product that is exactly what you want and keeping it within your set budget. Many times, you can purchase invitations printed for you for much less than you can make them, and this frees up a good deal of time and funds to focus on other tasks that will make your event more memorable.

Regardless of whether you opt for pre-made or handmade invitations, make sure they are addressed and in the mail **with the proper amount of postage** six-eight weeks prior to the wedding. If you send them out over two months in advance, it is likely they will be misplaced.

Take one completed invitation to the post office. If they are handmade and an odd size it could take a chunk out of your budget just to mail them and if you don't put proper postage you may get all your invitations back in the mail – ruined with all the stamps for insufficient funds.

Get clarity of when your invitations must be printed and delivered to you. Approximately three months in advance is sufficient to allow you time to address all your invitations, take one fully completed invitation to the post office to verify the amount of postage to be affixed, purchase the appropriate pretty love or theme stamp of your choice, and hand-write all the names and addresses on the outer and inner envelopes.

The inner envelopes are especially important if you are limiting the number of your invited guests to certain people in the household. For instance, Mr. & Mrs. Smith on the outside addressed envelope.

However, they have three children and you are only inviting the couple, you would write the first names of the Smith couple on the inner envelop to indicate exactly to whom this is an invitation to attend – such as John & Jane Smith

If you want to go a step further, you may want to place the words "Adults Only Please" discretely on the bottom of your printed invitation itself or print it on the RSVP card.

Now, if you are holding a themed wedding and you would really appreciate your guests showing up in "Island Attire" or "Black Tie" or "Masquerade," your invitations should reflect your desired dress code. Otherwise, you leave your guests with no direction calling each other asking "what do you think we should wear?" Help your guests out as much as possible. In today's busy and hectic lifestyles, no one has the time to ponder these thoughts at length. Many feel that this position is just too imposing on guests, while others, including myself, feel this honors your guests in the highest way.

Ambiguity serves no one.

Ceremony:

Prior to making plans on this subject, ask your ceremony venue what items they already have for your use as well as asking them what items may not be allowed due to stains from natural flower petals, wax drippings, possible fire, etc.

Some worship centers will not allow decoration outside of the flowers the bride and attendants carry, but some are equipped with a great number of accessories that you may utilize.

So the below assumes you are not at a venue that bans the use of excessive décor.

Aisle runner

Whether you decide to order the new aisle runners that have your monogram and faces printed on the fabric, or make your own, aisle runners can really pump up the volume on your theme and make the venue feel more customized to your particular taste.

If you want something super elaborate but still in the country, shabby-chic, or southern belle arena, how about purchase a bolt of burlap fabric and stitching silk petals into a pattern, then when it rolls out, you make a grand entrance.

On the aisle seating

Some bride's like having the end of every other row/pew have some sort of decoration. It can be a tall candelabra, a pail of flowers with fabric bows, a bouquet of flowers provided by your florist, or framed photos of the two of you growing up hanging on fabric loops. *(the progressive aging of the pictures of the bride on the left and groom on the right – going from baby to adulthood closer to the altar).*

Altar

Whether you utilize an arch, canopy, chuppah, a fire altar display, chairs, kneeling benches, ceremonial tables, towering floral displays, or simple trees, frame out the sacred place where you and your life partner will take your vows to one another. This should be a representation of your beliefs as well as the beliefs of your familial traditions – on both sides.

This is honoring where you both came from as well as where you will now go together. Families are more emotional about the ceremonies than even the bride and groom.

This is where you can negotiate implementing things for your family and get what you want for your reception.

Reception:

Tables for gifts, guest check-in, favors and/or table assignments

The gifts end up being decoration by themselves, but something has to start the collection. Regardless of how many times you have requested gifts to be sent to a specific address, they will still arrive at your reception and sometimes even your ceremony, so make sure you have a point-person to gratefully direct people where to place their gifts when they are presented without flinching or correcting the guest.

Have a visual aid that is tall yet narrow to denote *"this is the place"* to drop your gift off and it won't take up too much table space, so most of the gifts can fit on the table instead of on the floor.

There should be some sort of receptacle for collecting cards not attached to boxed gifts. Consider decorating a mailbox, birdcage, or lantern or purchasing a premade chest or decorated box with a slot the size of most envelopes.

Make sure there is someone that will guard the gifts during the reception, and once it is nearing a close, the bridesmaids, parents, or other designated people can transport the items to the couple's new home to await their return. Many times, you will need some extra spending cash for your honeymoon, and for security reasons, make sure someone gives the cards directly to you or your groom prior to your departure.

Many of the cards will have cash and/or checks inside. Open the envelopes and write the amount of cash or check there was inside on the back of the card for your thank you notes. Take the cash with you on the honeymoon or deposit it in the bank with the checks before you leave. Or use your best judgment that should be in charge of that detail *(which may need to wait until your return)*. You won't want to take all the cards with you on the trip since they could get lost on your trip – then someone's not getting a thank you note and that could cause hurt feelings.

Photo Booth or Backdrop

This is one of my favorite parts of a wedding. So many people want to commemorate getting all dolled up for a wonderful event and sometimes it is hard to find a spot where the background is pretty for a photo, or memorable for that matter.

Providing a lovely backdrop that fits with the flow of your theme will be a great feature for entertainment and memories of your guests. This area can also be a great conversation-starter for your guests to get to know each other and have an enjoyable time during the potential lulls between your arrival to the reception and your cake cutting.

A designated photographer tending the photo area is a great way to ensure you capture the festive nature of your guests.

Many technologies have been created for guests to capture their own pictures of your wedding-day events. The technology allows them to transport their photos to your wedding website. You and others who could not attend can review them and feel a part of your day as well.

Head Table or Table for 2

If you are thinking you would like to have a decorated sweetheart's table for just the two of you to have a private moment during dinner, this will allow your party to sit with their family and friends or significant others. However if you want to make sure your attendants don't drift off because you have a tight schedule to keep during the festivities, have the head table. Either way, decorate the fairydust out of it.

Your table should be still in keeping with the flow and theme; however, your table should also be very obvious. So go grand with your own backdrop, taller candelabras, or an elaborate table that needs no tablecloth, etc.

Go big!

Centerpieces

Centerpieces are an absolute essential for any major dinner – barring possibly Thanksgiving when a rather large turkey takes up the middle of the table. But centerpieces do not have to massively eat into your budget.

Just make certain your centerpieces are a direct representation of your theme and make a statement. When guests are confined to their tables for a good bit of the reception, it is important to have something pleasant and interesting to view and possibly something fun to create conversation between people who have never met before.

If you are having a rustic theme, get some large pails, wrap burlap around them, and fill with field flowers or baby's breath. Hang a few sepia-toned pictures of the two of you as a couple or even growing up. Write little known facts about how the two of you met or fell in love to help others feel more connected to the celebration of your love.

If you are doing a Gatsby style affair, rent some obnoxiously large candelabras that sport glittered taper candles, and string sparkling gemstone garland around the branches, put daisies and gem stones all around the rest of the table center.

Surrounding the cake

Make sure that the cake has its prominent spot, and that there is a nice screen, curtain or photo image behind the cake. After all, this is probably the most expensive food you will ever purchase in your lifetime. You want to make sure you have the perfect setting when your photographer snaps the shots of you and your newly-ringed-groom with this grand confectionary creation. There's is simply no appeal to a boring blank corner or wall or doorway taking up most of the space in the photo – much less an unintentional random photobomb person waiting to see cake smashed in your face and messing up your pictures.

Ask what sort of items the venue already has on-site to create a semi-circle approximately 3'– 4' behind the cake table *(so you can get between the cake and the background)*, if they have nothing, ask if you may hang something on the wall and if not, or bring in pipe and drape which does wonders for a beautiful backdrop. Just make sure the poles are decorated with something so they are not distracting. (this is a super-inexpensive backdrop to make if none is available for rental or on-site)

If you are on a super-restricted budget, make a balloon wall. You can pin balloons directly to a drape or a painted or wallpapered board. Just make sure the part that shows through the balloons meets with your theme and colors.

Seating

Assigned seats, assigned tables, or free-for-all general seating?

If you are planning to assign tables or even seats, you need some help with the seating chart before this time-consuming task can be completed. And when it is, how will you convey to your guests where they will be assigned?

Think table numbers, and seating cards with each individual's name. You need a display that will draw the eye as people filter into your reception room or beforehand at the cocktail hour. This display should flow with your theme, have cards with names and table designations printed clearly, and be in alphabetical order. How you choose to display your information is entirely up to you and your Bridesmaids.

Also, take a good look at the chairs themselves and decide if any additional décor needs to be added to them to either distract from their color or hide their wear and tear.

Dance floor

Sometimes, it is hard to know where the dance floor is in

a great ballroom at first glance until you get right up on it. So, here are a few ideas. Have your DJ light up the dance floor with a color wash blending with your theme.

Make a boarder or pattern with lanterns hanging from the ceiling. Have 200 helium balloons delivered with varying lengths of ribbons *(that you provided matching your theme)* tied to them, have one of your helpers bring fishing line and tie the ends of the balloons loosely together to form a large circle or square – this will make a boundary and you can release the rest of the balloons inside the boundary.

There are endless ideas of how to create something unique to your wedding, provide guidance to your guests, and have the party of a lifetime.

Hiring a Decorator

If you decide that your budget can handle a professional wedding decorator, do it! But before you dare to hire one, make sure you have seen quite a few pictures of past work.

Decorators are a different lot. You are not trying to gauge whether this person's personality works with yours. You *are* making certain this person's style will truly compliment your style and your theme and they *get* what you are describing to them. Decorator's work speaks for them, and one who can make something out of nothing with an endless imagination and good taste is like gold.

So, if you have found one you think is up to the task of creating what is in your imagination, get them to talk about the items below.

Questions

Is my date available for you to set-up and break-down the décor?

Ask to meet and interview the person who will be doing the decorating.

Ask to review photographs of their work. Clarify that the pictures that are provided are original works and not photographs from another designer.

Tell the designer your theme and what you had in mind. Gauge their level of excitement about your ideas and ask if they already possess decorations that would fit what you are dreaming.

Ask if they are able to make whatever you need they don't already have.

Ask for references.

Ask if the decorator has any special deals or other ways to give you the best value for your money.

List all your agreed décor requirements in the contract. Then ask the full amount you will pay, including all fees, before signing a contract.

Ask about the deposit amount and payment arrangements.

Ask for cancellation and refund policy.

A decorator may require a non-refundable deposit before agreeing to decorate your wedding, while another may establish a deadline after which the deposit becomes non-refundable. In most cases, once the decorator begins work, you're out the deposit.

Ask if the decorator will be responsible for removing and disposing of the decorations after the event. You may need to assign someone from your party, or put the clean-up of said items into the venue contract. But be sure to clarify who is responsible for clean-up.

Ask if there are any items that you will be able to keep or do all the decorations become the property of the decorator once the event is complete. If you want certain items, make sure to write it into the contract, or to have the decorator sign an amendment to the contract including the transfer of possession of said items.

MEMORIES

Toasts

Without a doubt, your maid(s) of honor and best man need to be prepared to toast you at the appropriate moment during the reception. But too many people making toasts can make your amazing day feel awkward, and like it is dragging along. So limit the number of people who will be handed the mic for toasting to your health. Many times, one or both of your parents will want to make a toast to you. Just make sure to ask them to not share specific things that you may not want made public.

The main thing is to set your personal expectation for a time limit.

Ask any of your toast-ers to keep their individual toasts timed between 30 seconds and one minute, that way even if one toast goes to two minutes, your reception will not feel the drag. Usually everyone is ready to take anyone's mic that goes over three minutes – unless they are just hilarious (to everyone) – so have someone on standby who will politely walk closer to them to relieve them of nervous rambling so the momentum keeps building and doesn't die.

Remind them they will be on camera which should help to curb anything they wouldn't want to really say ever again.

Guest Check-In

Guest registration has become an art form. No longer are we restrained by traditional little guest books that may be buried in a box and soon forgotten. You have the option of creating a piece of art to be displayed in your home that memorializes the attendance of all who witnessed your nuptials. You can collect well wishes from your guests on jenga blocks, or provide fun fact-finding games to your guests about you as a couple and then ask them for their marriage advice, have them sign the matting on the frame your wedding photo will be displayed in your home, or collect their thumbprints as the leaves of tree-art representing their stamp of approval on your union. The choices are endless for recording who honored you with their presence for your wedding and partied with you all night long afterward to celebrate.

Believe it or not, the day of your wedding will be an absolute blur and there is no way you can really process it all while it's happening. Having a memento of who attended is a great way to recapture memories that might have been lost completely.

Photographs & Video

Hindsight is 20/20: I'd hire a videographer, and I'd give more direction to the photographer

Photos and videos are your memories captured for years, decades, and even generations to come. The main point of the photographs is not really quantity but quality. How many pictures will you really hang on your wall? Now everyone needs a good assortment of photos to truly document the day. Because after the day is done you can barely remember what happened because you are in such a whirl. So make sure the professional you hire can deliver the well documented proof of your nuptials in the fashion you desire.

Most wedding photographers have a good assortment of their work on their websites, so many of your questions can be answered just by perusing through the gallery. However, you want to make certain they are the author of these pictures. If they are, point out the specific pictures you love the most and request you get "that" shot!

Again, make certain to look at the general pricing for each photographer and videographer to have an idea if you want to afford that much out of your budget. If you find their general pricing palpable, here are some very specific questions to ask while interviewing a few professionals that you are interested in hiring.

The majority of the following questions should be asked of both a photographer and videographer. There are only a few listed that are industry specific.

Do you have my date available?

(if they were recommended and you have not seen their work first hand)Do you have a portfolio I can review? Are all of the images yours, and is the work recent?

Why do you enjoy shooting weddings?

How many weddings have you shot? Have you done many similar to mine in size and style?

How would you describe your photography style (e.g. traditional, photojournalistic, romantic, creative)

What do you think distinguishes your work from that of other photographers?

When will the initial shots of my wedding be ready for my review?

Will you retouch the photos prior to printing my order? Is this an additional cost?

How long after I order my photos/album will I get them?

Will you give me the negatives or the digital images, and is there an additional fee for that?

Are you shooting in digital or film format or both?

Can I give you a list of specific shots we would like?

Will you put together a slideshow of the engagement session (along with other photos the couple provides) and show it during the cocktail hour? What about an "instant" slideshow of the ceremony?

What information do you need from me before the wedding day?

Have you ever worked with my florist, DJ, Coordinator, etc.?

May I have a list of references?

Are *you* the photographer who will shoot my wedding? If so, will you have any assistants with you on that day? If not, who will be taking the pictures and can I meet them before my wedding?

Do you have an assistant? How much more would it be to have both of you shooting the wedding?

How will you (and your assistants) be dressed?

Do you have a backup plan if you (or my scheduled photographer) are unable to shoot my wedding for some reason?

(If my wedding site is out of your area)Do you charge a travel fee and what does that cover?

Is it okay if other people take photos while you're taking photos?

Have you ever worked at my wedding site before? If not, do you plan to check it out in advance?

Are you photographing other events on the same day as mine?

What time will you arrive at the site and for how long or how many photos will you shoot?

Will you offer your services for my engagement photos?

Do you offer photographing a "first look" option within your packages?

What package would you recommend for what we have discussed today and what all does that include?

Can we customize a package to meet my specific needs?

How far in advance do I need to book with you?

What is the initial deposit to book the date?

If my event lasts longer than expected, will you stay? Is there an additional charge?

When can I expect a contract detailing what we have discussed? Can my specific shot requests be put into the contract?

What is your cancellation and refund policy?

Videographer only What formats can the final video be in?

Videographer only Do you offer demo DVDs for potential clients to look at?

Videographer only Do you have lighting equipment to accommodate a more dimly-lit event?

Videographer only What kind of equipment do you typically bring with you on the day of our wedding?

Videographer only Will you need access to an electrical outlet?

Is the client involved in the editing process? If so, how much input does the client have in editing?

Videographer only How long will our DVD be?

Videographer only What additional types of events do you service?

Videographer only Do you reserve the right to use the video in the future for promotional purposes?

Prior to Signing a Contract for a Photographer or Videographer, Ask Yourself:

Do I feel a good connection with this photographer as well as his/her photos/videos?

Are our personalities a good match?

Am I comfortable with this person's communication style?

Has he/she listened well and addressed all my concerns?

If you feel positive about your answers to these questions, book it!

Keep in mind that your guests will be taking a lot of candid shots throughout your day. Ask them to send those to you for your entertainment. Use your photographer to make sure you and your new spouse are looking your most fabulous with that glamorous and romantic twinkle in your eyes. That is the picture that will last throughout the decades to remind you of how much you love each other.

GIFTS

For Your Groom

Okay so it's your wedding day and your man is going to put everything aside that makes him comfortable just to make you happy. Whether it's putting on a tux, making a speech, doing a dance, or anything else that makes him uncomfortable, he's willing and committed to do it all for you just because you said "yes" to forever with him.

So, take this opportunity to be sweet to him. About a week before the wedding, shop for a gift "just for him" that would make him feel special and appreciated. Take the opportunity to write him a very sweet note telling him how much you love him and how you appreciate the way he has allowed you to have everything that is important to you. Have it waiting for him with a gift.

It doesn't matter how big or small the gift is or how long or short the note or letter is, just make sure this token of love and appreciation is a priority for that day. Show him that you respect something "he" loves enough to surprise him with it on your big day.

Whether your man is a fashionisto and a new pair of cuf-flinks would say I love you, or if you just put a pack of red Twizzlers in in his room with his favorite beverage.

Whatever works for him is what you should provide – especially if it is something you usually keep him away from – he will know you were thinking of "him" and love him.

Obviously, a fifth of jagermeister is not a good idea unless you want him tripping over his words at the altar.

If he has a specific place to get ready for the ceremony on-site, arrange for one of your valued friends to deliver it directly into his hands. Or, if you are doing a "first look" before the ceremony, present your gift to him in person after you blow his mind with your beauty, of course.

Any way you decide to do it, make sure he receives the gift directly in his hands by your hand or by a trusted courier so you will feel sure he has received it prior to the ceremony.

Also, make certain that he has had the opportunity for a private moment to read your message that conveys your love and respect for him as well as your excitement to see him looking all handsome.

For Your Attendants

Sometimes the best gifts for your attendants are the most obvious, like the jewelry they will wear for your wedding day. However, some brides love to pamper their girls and find individualized gifts they can use and remember your special relationship afterward as well.

If budget is no problem, you may want to treat all your girls to a spa day the weekend before or a few evenings before the wedding.

A bridesmaid luncheon is always a great way to bring the girls together for a big "thank you" and presenting your gifts, or if it is a really nice place, that outing might be the gift and you can present them with heart-felt hand written notes.

No matter what you decide to do, just make sure your girls feel as loved, appreciated, and pampered as they are going to make you feel the day of your wedding.

Registries

Face it. People want to bring you a gift of some kind to honor your new union. They may not be able to afford much or anything at all, and after all, that is not the point of inviting people to witness your marriage vows.

It is a courtesy in this fast-paced time to give your guests an idea of what you would be purchasing for yourself or what your plans are for your future, so if they are inclined to do so, they can contribute to your personal life goals instead of buying a random picture frame for you that you will undoubtedly re-gift.

However, do not have your registry information printed directly on your invitation. It sends the wrong message. Have an enclosed card that respectfully states that gifts are not expected, but if they were to give you something, please see option 1, 2 and 3 for what you would appreciate. Whether you are looking to renovate your new home together, trying to have a great honeymoon, or actually need household items, this enclosed card will give the guidance your guests need to select how to best help you.

Favors

Now, if you are cutting costs due to budget constraints, this is one costly place I would consider making the cut. Most people won't miss it, and no gift is better than a cheap stock gift that no one will ever use or look at again.

Qualify the quality of your gift as to whether you would want to receive it from someone else's wedding before making the purchase.

Consumables make great favors which is where the Jordan Almond tradition came from, however, M&Ms has been honing in on this market for a decade or more now with a vast array of colors. Wrappers and even candies can be imprinted with lettering or a photograph. Some consumables cost a little less than other favors and really do not require a lot of special packaging which cuts down on the cost and time to put them together.

However, if you want to do it up big, find a favor that strongly relates to your theme. If a lot of your friends are wine drinkers, there are great corkscrew favors to be had and the packaging or tag can flow with your theme.

Mini-wedding cakes, honey jars, measuring spoons, soaps, pie in a jar, and coffee are a few ideas to mull over as well.

THE MUSIC

Your choice of musical scores and emcees can make or break your ceremony and/or your party. Someone without good timing or stage presence or experience can really wreck the mood as well as your memories.

Make a list with your groom of songs that you both really like as well as a list of songs to avoid at all costs. If there is any emotional attachment to any particular music, it should be addressed privately as a couple and talked through so that your wedding day is only about celebrating your union without lingering memories of past relationships or old wounds.

Make sure the DJ gets this list in advance and again on the day of the wedding and be sure to reinforce that the do-not-plays are not negotiable under any circumstances including the requests of a guest. Put it in writing and have the DJ sign it. Also have a printed copy of that agreement for the DJ the day of the wedding as a refresher so there are no miscommunications or oops moments.

Now is the time when you decide if you can afford live musicians, a band, a DJ, a friend's iPod or a mix of the above.

Whether you have friends, or professionals, you need to make sure that your requests above are given to them in writing for the contract time as well as on the day of the wedding. If it is a friend, you need to clarify what is most important to you and not allow anyone that is not in full support of your vision to have the power to wreck your day.

Questions

May I see your playlist?

How many weddings have you done?

May I see video footage of a wedding/party where you have played, emceed, or DJ-d? *If you have already seen this footage, comment on what you like and would prefer for your event. Ask if you prefer a different tone if that is acceptable to that performer. Be sure to list your preferences in the contract!!!*

Are you available on my date?

I need you for "x" hours at my reception, or I need you just to play "x" songs for the ceremony, or I need you to play for the duration of the cocktail hour, etc. How much would you charge for what I need?

Ask how much the setup charge is, what it includes in addition to what you have asked for above. If this number is out of your remaining budget and you like this performer, ask if they can suggest any modification to what they normally provide in order to reduce the cost "because I would really like to have you at my wedding."

I would like it in writing what songs I am not willing to have played at my reception no matter what my guests request. Do you have a problem with that?

Side note:

You may need to pay a deposit to secure the date with performers, but get them to agree to receive the balance when they arrive at the ceremony/reception to perform their service.

Put in writing the time they should arrive, how they should be dressed, and who they should report to for guidance on where to setup. Make sure they receive their balance from that director when they arrive or they will be wondering if they will be getting paid at all.

SYMBOLISM

Rings

Your ring is your forever reminder of your decision to wed. It is the symbol of your love that says "I'm taken, keep movin' buddy." So your ring needs to be something you will be proud to wear and something without emotional attachment to anyone other than your spouse.

That said your ring is also something you should actually splurge on because it is what you will look at the most, every day, for the rest of your wedded life. This is the most important jewelry you will ever wear and needs to not be taken lightly. Now, I understand that there are budgets to keep in mind. If you decide to wear a ring that is handed down from a family member, try to make a new memory for it and give it some new meaning to go along with the nostalgia of the family keepsake.

However, if you can embrace spending a few extra bucks than what you would normally, have something made specifically for you, or shop with your betrothed for something you both like and make it a true symbol of your union. Put some good memories into it right away.

Design or purchase the rings together. Talk about the

sort of rings you would like prior to going shopping. And offer the jeweler some visual aids to help you in your search.

Select a reputable company and try on several different styles together and see what really speaks to you. Check to see if there is a financing option for what you want through that retailer and make certain you have arranged for financing or payment prior to shopping so you will know in which price range you need to remain.

For at least the first year, everyone is going to grab your hand and stare at your ring. Make sure you are comfortable with your selection and that it is a reflection of you and you are proud of what you are wearing.

If not, this one item can actually breed discontent in a marriage. It is ridiculous, but it is true. It is because it is with you every single day. It is not a wedding album that gets tucked into a drawer and you go weeks or months without looking at it. It is a constant, daily reminder of your union, your day, and your love. Make sure to make good memories surrounding this very important detail.

Unity Ceremony

Tying the knot, lighting the unity candle, blending sand or colored water in a vase, tea ceremony, or jumping the broom

These are a few options for your ceremony to show the union that has now been created between the two of you for the entire world to see. It may seem corny to some, but that just means you haven't chosen the symbol that best suits you as a couple. You may come up with your own unity symbol and start a new trend. But whatever you decide to do, it can be a very emotionally charged moment in the ceremony and that just shouldn't be missed by anyone.

Signing the Marriage License

In some ceremonies, there is a small desk off to the side and the bride and groom along with the witnesses sign the marriage license after exchanging their vows during the ceremony.

Depending on how you structure it, this could be a very powerful moment or a very awkward one. Make sure you plan exactly how you will do this logistically if you want to incorporate it into your ceremony.

It does seem to make things more real and official with that piece of paper staring you in the face. Maybe more couples should do it and they would take their marriage vows a little more seriously.

Many times the marriage certificate has actually gone unsigned until the end of the evening or until the couple returns from honeymoon. Note: You aren't legally married until it is signed and the officiant turns it into the courthouse and you receive your marriage certificate in the mail. If you don't believe me, try having your name changed on anything without it.

Cultural Ceremonies & Family Tradition

Remember to include traditions from your individual origins and find great ways to blend in important family and religious traditions. For some this is a stretch but understand that this is where you have the opportunity to allow your families the joy they would also like to have for your big day. Even if some things are meaningless to you, they have very deep roots within the emotional gene pool.

You can come out on top if you are willing to give in on items that don't mean that much to you if they mean the world to those you love.

The ceremony is a great time to take care of these things and then the reception can be the party you always dreamed of.

Honoring Those Who Have Passed

Sometimes we miss important people from our families and those whose absence left holes in our lives. If you or your groom have lost a loved one that you really wish could have been there to witness your happiness, create a small memorial for them on the front row and possibly on a table at the reception. You can even mention who the memorials are for within the program if you make those memorials part of the ceremonial walk down the aisle.

Some brides wear a memento from their loved one or a charm with their picture in their bouquet. Memorials can include a candle lit just prior to the ceremony. Some are comprised of pictures of the departed.

However you choose to honor your loved ones, it will make you feel more like you were able to share this special moment with them and make your day feel more complete.

Giving Away the Bride

There is probably more controversy and drama around this one ceremonial bit than any other, so let's address it right now.

Back when women were property and bargaining tools, the father would escort the bride to the altar, sometimes along with her entire family. Yes, the bride was escorted by more than one person and even a crowd in tow. Many cultures still actually practice this, not to make sure the bride doesn't run off anymore, but to show their public support for the union.

If you want to honor to your father because you have an

amazing relationship and you're a daddy's girl go for it, or if your mother actually raised and provided for you, have her walk you down the aisle. If you want to have both your fathers or mothers, or brother walk you, or be bold and walk alone and present yourself to the one you love – do it.

The other part of this ceremony is "Who gives this woman to be wed?..." , "Who gives their blessing on this union?", etc. insert wording here...

If you want super-traditional because it is what you always dreamed of, go with your parent or set of parents at the altar or rising from their seats and saying in unison "I do" or father says "her mother and I" or all your parents can state "we do." How about having the officiant address the whole crowd and ask, "Who gives their blessing to this union?" "If you support this couple, you all may respond by saying "I do"" showing the couple the amount of support they have toward a successful marriage. Ooooo. I like that!

ACTIVITIES

Showers

You may end up with more than one shower if you have close friends in more than one city or state, or if you have a very diverse set of friends. Now, if more than one person has asked to give a shower, here are some things to consider.

Do these girls even know each other or are they from different areas of my life? If they are close, ask if they can co-host and join forces, however, if they do not know each other, let the secondary know that someone is giving you a shower from (wherever you know them from) and ask if she would like to be invited to that shower or if she would still like to throw her own. If you decide to allow her to throw a separate shower for you, make sure that individuals are not invited to both showers unless you have a close mutual relationship that would want to attend both events and not feel obligated to bring you two gifts.

No matter if you have one or multiple showers; here are some questions to ask the person offering to give you a shower.

What date(s) were you considering for the shower?

Are only girls invited or were you planning a "Jack and Jill" party that lets the guys join in?

Who are the people you had in mind to invite?

What type of shower will this be?

Do you want me to make a designated gift registry somewhere for this specific party?

Where were you thinking about holding the party?

Bachelorette Party

Destination? Stripper? Alcohol? Pole Dancing Demonstration and Lessons? Lingerie? or Naughty Toy Night? These are usually questions you want to think about when giving guidance to whomever is throwing your Bachelorette party, which is traditionally your Maid of Honor; however, it does not have to be her.

You may want to reference some of the same questions listed in the shower section.

The Bachelor and Bachelorette parties start more arguments and breed more animosity than any other party thrown – ever.

However, you can navigate the drama by keeping open communication and letting your wishes be clear. Remember, you have the mate of your dreams wanting to spend the rest of his life with you on the other side of this party.

Be careful of what you allow your host(ess) to throw at you. If you have very strong opinions about some type of entertainment or activity being excluded, you need to be very clear about your feelings at the beginning with that person. If you find they don't respect your wishes after you have specified your preferences, you may want to re-consider their motives and friendship and possibly not be as close to them after your wedding.

This party is right before your wedding, so now is not the time for drunken brawls or major drama. Keep is classy. Your friend may be misguided or have unre-solved issues about you tying the knot or whom you are tying it with. Try to give them the benefit of the doubt if it was an innocent slip-up.

Bachelor Party

You do not want to end up with a missing groom the day of your wedding. Just keep this in mind and keep a few tabs on what your man has planned or his best man has planned or that devious cousin of yours has planned.

You may want to request that the bachelor party be scheduled for the weekend a full week prior to your wedding for the above reasons. You know who the bad influencers are on your man. Take appropriate precau-tions but don't spy on them.

For Out of Town Guests

Depending on when your guests will arrive and how much time you realistically want to spend with them, it may be nice to schedule some fun events to enjoy your friendships and family connections.

If your city of choice offers a few touristy activities, if there is golf or mini-golf, skiing, or even a lake or beach front restaurant, there are usually a few activities or gatherings you can schedule two months prior to the wedding.

You want to make certain to do this prior to your invitations being mailed so you can include a special insert specifically for your out-of-town guests so they can plan accordingly and offer an RSVP for the suggestions.

Remember to make suggestions for hotel accommodations and if the number of out-of-town-ers is great, reserve a small block of rooms at the most convenient hotel to your event. Then convey that information in an insert to the invitation.

Make sure to check back with the hotel to see if your guests have indeed booked rooms there. You may need to deliver the finalized itinerary to their rooms along with a welcome basket as a thank you for making the trip and spending the necessary funds to attend your big celebration.

Morning After Brunch

It is a lovely gesture to schedule a brunch to thank your parents, wedding party, people that went above and beyond the day of your wedding, as well as your out-of-town guests for making the trip. It is rare that you get the opportunity to see some people and it is a great time to have conversations with the people you love that don't end with a to-do list because the main event is over.

This will give you some relaxed time with the people closest to you where you can begin reminiscing over the previous day's events. This also allows you a reprieve to enjoy a night or two and a day before leaving for your honeymoon trip.

GETTING THERE

You don't necessarily have to splurge on a limo or horse-drawn carriage, but you do need to arrive at your wedding in some way, so let's address the moving parts that apply to every couple. Whether you drive yourself or go all out with multiple chauffeurs, you need to make a plan and inform the appropriate people of your plan.

If you are hiring a limousine service, make sure to hire a reputable transportation company and to ask for non-smoking vehicles if you do not want to arrive smelling like smoke. Whether your style is suited by a classic Rolls-Royce, a Hummer stretch or a sweetheart limo with a heart-shape Jacuzzi on the back, make the most of your moments riding in these luxurious automobiles you have chosen.

Make sure you understand all the charges included in these rentals. If there is an hourly rate, an additional fuel charge, or fees for swapping out vehicles for each leg of the event, make sure you know the total bill before signing the contract and putting this into your budget.

If you are hiring a horse and carriage, make certain to find out the distance they are willing to travel.

You may need to meet them somewhere close by in a car

and have them bring you to the front door of your ceremony venue if you are choosing a grand entrance.

Remember that if you are on a super budget, most people are not going to see you arrive because they are already inside the church waiting for you to walk the aisle – unless you follow another culture and everyone waits outside the venue until you arrive and then goes inside to secure their seats.

However, if you have just been pining for the horse and buggy all your life, make it count and have them pick you up from the ceremony or the reception to whisk you away to your wedding night bliss.

What a romantic way to go. Again, make sure to address all the details with your charter because I doubt they will be taking you to the airport hotel from 50 miles away in a carriage.

Take a moment to dream and pencil in your thoughts about how regal or glamorous or simple you want to make your transportation details using the categories below.

Use it as a guide going forward to make your plans and be sure your day-of coordinator knows this information.

Other items to think of:

How will your party arrive?

How will both sets of parents arrive?

How will your party be transferred from the ceremony to the reception *(if separate locations)*?

Even if the answer is personal car, write that down. If it is a hired service, note the name of the service along with the phone number, exact agreed upon time and location of pickup. Have a copy of this with you. Be sure to give one to your groom, your maid of honor, and even your parents if you are also arranging their transportation.

Make certain you understand if the gratuity for the driver is in the agreed payment for service. If not, set aside an envelope with a cash tip for the driver(s) to be given on that day. Give this to your most organized attendant to distribute.

The following is a list of your categories for which you will need some sort of transportation.

Getting to the Ceremony
Ceremony to Reception
Leaving the Reception
Transportation to Wedding Night Accommodations
Transportation to Honeymoon
Transportation back Home

THE DAY BEFORE

So, here's some last minute preparation.

Make one box for going to the Ceremony Venue

Emergency Kit:
Alcohol
Peroxide
Cotton balls
Q tips
Pain relievers
Bandaids
Scissors
Needle and thread in gown and bridesmaid colors
Hairspray, comb, bobby pins
Deodorant, toothbrush and toothpaste
Writing pen, notecards/envelopes
Battery-operated portable fan w/batteries
Lipstick you and bridesmaids wear tomorrow
Nail polish you and bridesmaids wear tomorrow
Phone charger along with any other electronic items you
will be taking with you

Marriage License *(officiant and two adult witnesses signatures usually needed to make it legal)*

Guest book and designated writing utensils *(make sure someone is assigned to get this from the ceremony to the reception)*

Two copies of all your announcements and invitations to each event leading up to and including the wedding *(photographer and videographer each get a set)*

Payment for officiant

Payment for musicians and/or DJ and/or sound coordinator and any other lingering vendors who haven't been paid in full

Gratuity for chauffeurs along with gratuities for any other vendors you wish to thank beyond their charged services *(make sure these are in cash in individually sealed and marked envelopes) (have one designated person responsible for distributing)*

Make one box for going to the <u>Reception Venue</u>

Going away clothing for you and him

Favors

Cake knife and server

Toasting flutes, pictures of loved ones that have been honored because they have passed on, other breakables – *bring in, keep, and repack in the original packaging to avoid damage or breakage*

Confirm who is transporting the boxes back to your home.

THE BIG DAY

Ok, so here we are! Congratulations!

Despite the fact there is still a great deal to do today, it is now time to allow others to take the reins. Your time is done – well mostly.

You still have to show up all done up and get to the altar on-time. That's enough to overload someone who is probably emotionally-fragile at this point – namely you!

You've done a good job orchestrating everything, setting up your people to take charge of important details. Now, it is your job to take an emotional step back. Enjoy the day as it unfolds. It will go by in a blink.

Do your best to savor every special moment and not rush anything. And if by chance anything doesn't go exactly as you planned – and if you actually notice – decide to be happy just as if you planned it that way.

Sometimes, we can think things through a thousand ways and know we planned for "that," but "something like that" happens anyway and quite frankly, there's nothing you can do about it at this point. Some of those things can work in your favor just the same.

So sit back and decide that no matter what, you'll just roll with it and act like it was planned that way. Your guests most likely won't know any different unless you tell them there was a problem.

Smile! Be Happy! It is the right choice!
And remember, it is YOUR choice!

YOUR HONEYMOON

A honeymoon is all in the planning. This is one of the most amazing times of your life. It is a time you can revel in the words "husband" and "wife." This should be one of the most magical times in your life. A time you can reflect on with your spouse for decades to come. Make the most of it!

Now, if you have spent all your dough on your nuptials, it will be hard to pull together a world-class trip; however, if you have smartly budgeted, you can have both your cake and party it off too....

Even if all you have left is enough to spend a few nights at a bed & breakfast an hour or two away. Take the time and money to do it.

Regret for not having any sort of honeymoon is a long-lingering thing. Don't put that sort of pressure on your marriage.

Rental Car
Bed & Breakfast
Theme Park
Airfare
Passport
Cruise

If you are already planning on the honeymoon of a life-time, check the expiration date on your current passports as soon as you get engaged and begin dreamy thoughts of faraway places in the world to visit to celebrate and display your love.

This little legal matter of a valid passport could limit your choices very quickly if you don't address this issue right away. If the expiration date will fall during your honeymoon or before the wedding or if either of your passports is already expired, make sure to download the renewal form (or order form if either of you has never had a passport), get some new mug shots taken at the local drugstore offering passport photos and take in or send in your applications right away.

Go to travel.state.gov/passport for the forms and guide-lines you will need to complete your first or renewal application.

If you don't do it right at the beginning, you could really regret it later. Estimate paying approximately $150 per person. They do have an additional fee for rush service available under $100 each if you need to have your application processed very quickly (be warned: passport applications can take as long as several months!)

As soon as the new passports arrive, scan them (or your current ones) into an attachment and email them to yourself (and your groom), print a color photocopy of them to place inside your checked luggage.

Also, go a step further and download the attachments to

your smartphones and tablets. In the event you are separated from your documents and unable to access the internet, you will have the scanned image of your documents handy for identification purposes and to show your local embassy should there be a problem.

Be sure your driver's licenses are up to date and your original passports are packed safely in the outside compartment of your ***carry-on luggage***. You will need immediate access to these items several times. Travel check-in and security will not let you get on the plane or cruise with expired identification.

Also, keep in mind that if you stay in a hotel in another country, you must surrender your passport for the key to your room. This is common and can be a little scary initially, but abroad, hotels are responsible for knowing exactly who is in their hotel at all times.

In the future, we will be adding a honeymoon travel vlog and honeymoon packages to www.FairyBridemother.com.

If you subscribe, and get your bonus to this book, you will also get all updates on services, products, and promotions that will be offered in the future.

Make sure to opt-in to the honeymoon help list when it comes available.

If you are already subscribing to FairyBridemother's YouTube channel, there will most definitely be announcements on the videos.

If not, follow this link to the YouTube channel and subscribe.

WHAT NOW?
THE RETURN "HOME?"

Probably one of the biggest hurdles in a marriage is at the very beginning, the return to normality.

But nothing is normal now.

There are two sets of stuff and now it is time to figure out how to merge lives so there is less friction when you return in your blissfully happy state of mind.

Whether that means selling most everything you already owned as single people and selecting new furnishings as a couple, or if it means trying to figure out how to blend two completely opposing styles into one "home." Make the major decisions before you wed and head off to honeymoon-land.

First things First

Write and address your thank you notes to the people that sent you gifts, gave you their time and/or talents for free *(or a reduced cost),* paid for any part of your wedding, arranged for you to get services for a discount or free, gave you gifts of money, as well as to your attendants and remember your parents.

This should be done almost immediately out of courtesy for the above mentioned. It is a huge task. These notes do NOT need to be long. They just need to be done.

"Thank you for just being by my side to help me pull off the wedding of my dreams. Your support meant every-thing to me and ____."

Get it? Enclosing a nice picture of the two of you on the wedding day or from your honeymoon is a lovely touch. Make the picture unframed and normal size (4x6); how-ever, you may want to choose a lovely frame that match-es the style and taste of your parent's homes for a 5x7 as their keepsake.

Designate two hours at least one night a week until all the necessary notes are completed.

Schedule it!

Secondly

As soon as you have thanked your guests, thank your vendors with a glowing online review and a grateful email sent directly to them.

Your endorsement of that vendor is crucial because it helps others to decide whether or not to hire the vendors you chose.

Your honest feedback in a private email is very im-portant because it helps to make your vendor even bet-ter!

Make sure you have done this within two months after returning from your honeymoon. With one caveat – wait until you receive the final product on your photography and videography, etc. prior to giving that glowing recommendation.

If you had a problem, address it directly with the vendor first and allow them to respond and/or make it right prior to leaving negative feedback.

Thirdly

After your thank you notes and reviews are done, it is time to get into married life – full swing.

A great way to start this off is not to lose the element of dating. Set aside a night a week just to be together without any real agenda – unless it's a date night where you take turns planning an evening for each other.

Make this a night where it is just about the two of you. Even if all you do is share a meal and communicate, that's a great way to keep the health of your relationship a priority!

Keep the love alive. Marriage is work, but it can be much easier by laying the proper foundations and expectations early on.

If you haven't already done so, please look for my next book, *FairyBridemother's Dating, Love & Marriage Handbook.*

Side Notes

And if you really wish a lot of this planning stuff was already automated and there were new magic ways for you to communicate with everyone involved in your planning – for you and brides to come, we're working on that too.

The proceeds from this book and Bride Bootcamps are going to fund just that. If you would like to see it done faster, you may contribute to the cause at www.CircleWhite.com

I certainly hope this information has been helpful in planning your big day.

I would love to know how it helped!
www.FairyBridemother.com

Happy Planning,

Fairy Bridemother

P.S. I've added a yummy cerebral snack for those of you who always wanted the scoop on how traditions got started. Go to www.Fairy-Bridemother.com/bonus to collect and connect with me.

137

139

The concept of FairyBridemother is directly from the mind of Melinda Morgan in 2012. She was originally created and designed solely to be the guide through www.CircleWhite.com as a helper, educator, and entertainer.

FairyBridemother, CircleWhite, nor FairyTale Publishing, Inc. are responsible for the actual outcome of your event. This book is meant to guide you along your individual path. The choices you make are yours alone.

Proceeds from the sale of this book are going to initially fund the creation of www.CircleWhite.com. The primary vision for these companies is to create better communication skills, help to set better boundaries, help to facilitate the creation of fabulous events everywhere, and with great dreams, hopes and prayer, successfully reduce the divorce rate.

This book is the first guide released to accomplish this overall vision.

Thank you for your support.